"This is simply a great workbook. Although written for teens, it will prove valuable for others, too: as self-help for adults, as an adjunct to treatment for therapists, and as a guide for parents of younger children. Tompkins and Barkin teach you powerful skills in a highly readable and interesting way, using real-life examples and step-by-step instructions. It will be so worth it to work through the exercises. You will undoubtedly reduce your stress, increase your well-being, and significantly improve your life."

> —**Judith S. Beck, PhD**, president of the Beck Institute for Cognitive
> Behavior Therapy

"I'm so stressed!' The average age of my clients is about sixteen years old and I hear those words all too frequently. I know that I will be recommending this workbook to my clients (though I believe adults will find it equally helpful). It is accessible, on point, and very engaging! I also really like the pacing of the activities. This book is a wonderful resource! Thank you, Tompkins and Barkin."

> —**Joan K. Orrell-Valente, PhD**, former assistant professor in the Division
> of Adolescent and Young Adult Medicine at the University of California,
> San Francisco; currently in private practice in San Francisco, CA

"In *The Relaxation and Stress Reduction Workbook for Teens*, Tompkins and Barkin provide a masterful, clearly written book to help teens effectively cope with anxiety and stress. In a time in which so many teens are experiencing distress, this book promises to be a highly useful resource for its readers."

> —**Eric Storch, PhD**, All Children's Hospital Guild Endowed Chair
> Professor in the departments of pediatrics (primary), health policy and
> management, psychiatry and neurosciences, and psychology at the
> University of South Florida

"This is a hands-on, useful, and well-written workbook. The text and exercises are useful, clear, and written in an accessible way. This book will help teens build their capacity for dealing with anxiety and stress while developing skills and healthy habits that will have lifelong benefits. I will be recommending this to parents and teens frequently, in addition to using some of the techniques myself."

> —**Nelson Branco, MD, FAAP**, pediatrician at Tamalpais Pediatrics in
> Larkspur, CA; and assistant clinical professor of pediatrics at the
> University of California, San Francisco

"Adolescence is becoming an increasingly stressful time for young people, and valuable resources are needed by teenagers as well as the professionals who care for them. *The Relaxation and Stress Reduction Workbook for Teens*—expertly written by Tompkins and Barkin—powerfully fulfills this important mission. This is a comprehensive tool kit which makes the empirically based skills for mitigating stress in young patients accessible to teens and clinical providers through engaging text material, compelling exercises, and actionable forms. The workbook is an invaluable resource prepared by master clinicians that will be reached for again and again to help stressed-out teenagers."

> —**Robert D. Friedberg, PhD, ABPP**, professor and director at the Center for the Study and Treatment of Anxious Youth at Palo Alto University

"Adolescents and young adults seem to be more stressed than ever. Now, there is a book that offers relief. The strategies in this workbook have been studied by researchers and used by therapists for decades, and here they are presented in an accessible, easy-to-digest format designed specifically for teens. The book is engaging and filled with helpful activities. Readers will learn tried-and-true strategies for calming their minds and relaxing their bodies. Any teen who feels stressed out by the challenges of school, friendships, family, money, or other areas of life should check out this book!"

> —**Martin M. Antony, PhD**, professor of psychology at Ryerson University, and coauthor of *The Shyness and Social Anxiety Workbook* and *The Anti-Anxiety Workbook*

"This book is an excellent resource for clinicians. It is chock-full of easy-to-understand-and-apply lessons that can be used as handouts for therapy clients. It can also be used as a self-help book for motivated teens struggling with anxiety. I recommend it highly!"

> —**Mary A. Fristad, PhD, ABPP**, professor of psychiatry, psychology, and nutrition at The Ohio State University, and member of the Neuroscience Research Institute

"In these pressured times we live in, every teen is a stressed teen, but it doesn't have to be that way. Now more than ever, teenagers need tools to take charge of what can feel like the runaway train of worry. Stress may be a part of life, but teenagers are eager for relief. They just need to know what works. In *The Relaxation and Stress Reduction Workbook for Teens*, young people will quickly find easy-to-incorporate, effective tools to make a difference in the way they see their lives, and live their lives. Parents will do well to pick up a copy for their teen (and borrow some strategies for themselves)!"

> —**Tamar Chansky, PhD**, author of *Freeing Your Child from Anxiety* and *Freeing Your Child from Negative Thinking*

the relaxation & stress reduction workbook for teens

cbt skills to help you deal with worry & anxiety

MICHAEL A. TOMPKINS, PhD
JONATHAN R. BARKIN, PsyD

Instant Help Books
An Imprint of New Harbinger Publications, Inc.

For Ainsley, Madeleine, Abby, and Olivia—girl power galore.

—MAT

For Hannah and Owen, who one day will be old enough to read this dedication.

—JB

Publisher's Note

Distributed in Canada by Raincoast Books

Copyright © 2018 by Michael A. Tompkins and Jonathan R. Barkin
        Instant Help Books
        An imprint of New Harbinger Publications, Inc.
        5674 Shattuck Avenue
        Oakland, CA 94609
        www.newharbinger.com

Cover design by Amy Shoup

Acquired by Tesilay Hanauer

Edited by Karen Schaeder

Library of Congress Cataloging-in-Publication Data on file

20   19   18

10 9 8 7 6 5 4 3 2 1   First Printing

contents

Foreword   vii

To Teens Reading This Workbook   ix

Section I
You Say You're Stressin' but What Does That Mean?

Activity 1. Your Sources of Stress   2

Activity 2. How You Cope with Stress   6

Activity 3. Creating Your Game Plan   10

Activity 4. Keeping a Stress Diary   13

Section II
Relaxing Your Stressed-Out Body

Activity 5. Slow Deep Breathing   20

Activity 6. Progressive Muscle Relaxation   25

Activity 7. Shifting into Automatic Relaxation   29

Section III
Focusing Your Attention to Relax Your Stressed-Out Mind

Activity 8. Meditation   34

Activity 9. Mindfulness: Five-Senses Awareness   38

Activity 10. Visualization   42

Section IV
Working Your Way Through Worry

Activity 11. Your Sources of Worry   46

Activity 12. Your Thinking Mistakes   51

Activity 13. The Key Question: Where's the Evidence?   54

Activity 14. Overthrowing the Tyranny of "Should"   58

Activity 15. Following the Path of Value   62

Section V
Working Your Way Through Fear

Activity 16. Building a Plan to Work Your Way Through Fear   66

Activity 17. Building Your Act-Brave Ladder   70

Activity 18. Putting Your Working-Your-Way-Through-Fear Plan to the Test   75

Activity 19. Imagining Your Way Through Fear   79

Section VI
Solving the Problems in Your Life So That You Don't Stress About Them

Activity 20. Identifying the Problem (and That's Not Always Easy)   82

Activity 21. Brainstorming Possible Solutions and Keeping
              an Open Mind   85

Activity 22. Examining the Pluses and Minuses and Deciding
              What to Try First   89

Activity 23. The Power of Constructive Worry   94

Section VII
Communicating Clearly and Saying No

Activity 24. Clear Communication Begins with Good Listening   98

Activity 25. Clear Communication Includes I-messages   102

Activity 26. Clear Communication Sends the Correct Message   106

Activity 27. Four Steps to Saying No   109

Section VIII
Putting It off Just Heaps It on

Activity 28. Breaking It Down to Move Things Along   114

Activity 29. Cutting a Corner to Move Things Along   117

Activity 30. Procrastinating Less to Stress Less   120

Section IX
Managing Stress That Angers You So You Can Manage Anger That Stresses You

Activity 31. Your Sources of Anger   126

Activity 32. Identifying Your Anger Stages   131

Activity 33. Using Coping Thoughts and Actions to Cool Down   135

Activity 34. Creating Your Anger Management Plan and Putting It to the Test   139

Section X
Eating Right, Eating Well—Just Try Not to Eat to Calm Down

Activity 35. Your Eating Right, Eating Well Profile   144

Activity 36. Developing Your Eating Right, Eating Well Plan   147

Section XI
Exercising Your Way to Less Stress

Activity 37. Selecting the Best Exercise for You   152

Activity 38. Developing Your Exercise Plan   155

Section XII
Space Matters: Creating a Calm Environment

Activity 39. Creating a Calming Space   162

Activity 40. Harnessing the Power of Your Calming Space   166

Wrapping Up   168

Acknowledgments   169

foreword

People generally acknowledge that—and research supports this—we face more stress as teens than at any other time in life. Teens confront huge challenges, threats, and demands in a world where they have very little control. This is, in fact, the recipe for high stress: lots of risk and little control.

Much has been learned and written about teen stress, but next to nothing has been written *for* teens *with* stress. Until now, with *The Relaxation & Stress Reduction Workbook for Teens*. The focus of this extraordinary book is not on concepts related to stress, or an exploration of how bad teen stress is. Teens know how bad it is. The focus is on specific, proven-effective tools to turn the knob down on physical, cognitive, and emotional distress: tools for feeling better in the face of fear and pressure and things that feel out of control.

Stress doesn't get better from thinking or learning about it; it gets better with doing something about it. This workbook is about throwing water on the fire; it's about evidence-based strategies and activities that reduce teen stress and overwhelm and make it possible for teens to feel fully engaged with life.

Almost forty years ago, Martha Davis, Patrick Fanning, and I wrote the original *Relaxation & Stress Reduction Workbook* for adults. Our aim was to collect from the scientific literature the most efficacious techniques for arousal reduction. Readers could be confident that these techniques worked, and as they practiced the strategies, they could discover which ones worked best *for them*.

The same philosophy lies at the heart of *The Relaxation & Stress Reduction Workbook for Teens*. Each activity is supported by scientific research. Each activity offers a specific coping tool that is carefully adapted for youth. Each activity gives teens a path to stress relief and inner calm.

There are many sources of stress. Authors Michael Tompkins and Jonathan Barkin start by helping readers assess the drivers for their own stress reactions, whether those are physical tension, cognitive processes such as worry or perfectionism, specific fears, environmental stressors, procrastination, intense emotions, or some other source of stress. Then, for each potential source of stress, the book offers easy-to-do activities that build a particular stress-management skill. Chronic body tension, for example, is targeted with breathing and muscle release skills. Cognitive stress is addressed with mindfulness, positive visualizations, and activities to promote more realistic and healthy thinking. Fear is targeted with activities designed to help teens face things they avoid, so they can build their lives around acceptance and what they value rather than running away.

A whole suite of problem-solving and communication skills are offered to help with interpersonal and environmental stressors. Three activities focus on overcoming procrastination, a huge source of teen stress. Surging emotions, particularly anger, plague youth; Drs. Tompkins and Barkin provide activities to help teens recognize the sources of their anger and develop a unique anger management plan. Diet, exercise, and the development of calming personal space are also emphasized.

The Relaxation & Stress Reduction Workbook for Teens is the best resource available for teen stress. This comprehensive, science-based, user-friendly volume offers the skills teens need to lighten the burden of physical, cognitive, and emotion-driven stress.

—Matthew McKay, PhD
Coauthor, *The Relaxation & Stress Reduction Workbook*

to teens reading this workbook

If you're reading this workbook, it's likely someone who cares about you thinks you might be stressed, and that someone might be right. Teens report that their stress levels during the school year are much higher than they believe is healthy. Furthermore, their stress levels are even higher than adults'. Stressed teens often feel overwhelmed, depressed, or sad. Stress has a big effect on the health of teens, too. Stressed teens tend to exercise less, sleep less, and eat more unhealthy foods.

Yes, stress is serious business when you're a teen, but you can learn to relax and manage your stress, and the activities in this workbook can help you do that. You'll learn activities to help you shift into relaxation and calm your body and mind. You'll learn activities to help you manage your worry, if you tend to worry too much. You'll learn activities to help you stop procrastinating and communicate better with friends, teachers, and family members; and you'll learn to keep your eye on the basics—nutrition and exercise. Many of the activities include worksheets that are also available for download at http://www.newharbinger.com/40095; at the back of this book, you'll find details about accessing these downloads. It will take some time and practice to master the activities in this workbook, but once you learn them, you'll feel more on top of things and better about yourself.

This workbook will not take the place of counseling. Some teens benefit from the added support of a counselor as they learn and practice the activities in the workbook. A counselor can also help you select the activities that are the best fit for you and for what you're dealing with. Speak to your parents if you think a counselor could help you.

We hope you'll learn and practice the activities in this workbook. Once you learn them, you'll use them over and over throughout your life. We do.

You Say You're Stressin' but What Does That Mean?

1 your sources of stress

for you to know

A teen's life is stressful. There are tests, friendships, dating, and college applications, to name a few. Every teen is different so the way your best friend handles stress may differ from how you handle stress. The first step in learning to relax and reduce your stress is to identify the things that tend to stress you out in the first place.

Roxanna is stressed about the math test that is coming up this Friday. She studies every night, but with soccer tryouts and her other homework, she can't study as much as she wants. She feels unprepared and in a panic. Sydney, on the other hand, never seems to stress about tests or homework. She just gives them a good effort and accepts that she may not be able to study as much as she needs to. What does stress her out is her friendships and, more recently, how her mom and dad are not getting along.

for you to do

This activity helps you identify the things that tend to stress you out. Place a check next to all the stressful events or situations that apply to you.

Stressful Event or Situation	√
Family (for example, your parents are divorcing or separating, your parents are arguing with each other or with you, you're having regular conflicts with your brothers or sisters)	
School or academics (for example, tests, grades, difficult teachers, having a different learning style)	
Friendships (for example, regular conflicts with your friends, betrayals, loss of friendships, friends asking you to keep secrets)	
Body image (for example, you're overly concerned about your weight, height, hair, skin blemishes, ethnicity)	
Romantic relationships (for example, new relationship, recent breakup, complicated relationship, having very different expectations for the relationship)	
Bullying or cyberbullying (for example, other people are repeatedly humiliating you in front of other teens or adults, you're the target of hurtful comments or photos)	
Peer pressure (for example, other teens regularly pressure you to use drugs or alcohol, have sex, or take other risks)	
Money or resources (for example, you and your family don't have enough money to buy books, to pay for school uniforms or attend school functions and clubs, to buy clothes and other things that would help you fit in with your friends and other teens)	
Change (for example, you're moving to a different house or school, a new sibling was just born, you lost your pet, a grandparent, or a close friend)	

The list doesn't contain every possible situation or event that stresses out teens. These are just typical examples of sources of teen stress. Stress can build over time. Events or situations that happened to you two or more years ago can still be stressing you out. Many of the activities you'll learn in the workbook will help you feel less stressed about those things, too. On the lines below, write the events or situations that are stressing you out now, or have stressed you out in the past, but don't appear in the list.

_____

_____

_____

_____

_____

_____

more to do

Many times, the situations that stress teens the most are situations they don't have much control over. For example, you don't have much control over whether your parents argue with each other. If your parents decide to move to another city, you don't have much control over whether you and your family move. What you *do* have control over is how you respond to these things. Many of the activities you'll learn in the workbook will help you feel a bit more in control of your stress and your life.

Think about the stressful situations in your life now, and in the past, that you wish you had control over, and write them on the lines below.

_____

_____

_____

_____

_____

_____

2 how you cope with stress

for you to know

Teens cope with stress in different ways. Some ways are healthier than others. For example, one teen might cope with stress by binge-watching shows and videos; another might hang out with friends more. Many times, teens fall into a pattern of coping with stress in unhealthy or negative ways because they have never learned healthy or positive ways to cope.

for you to do

The first step to increasing the number of healthy ways you cope with stress is to take a look at both the healthy and unhealthy ways you cope with stress now. Below is a list of the positive (healthy) and negative (unhealthy) ways teens typically cope with stress. A positive way is one that improves your physical, social, or emotional well-being; for example, going for a run or connecting with friends. A negative way is one that undermines your well-being. This can involve avoiding the problem that is stressing you out altogether, such as putting off studying for a math test because you're worried you might fail. Habits that get out of hand, such as bingeing on junk food or staying up late streaming videos or gaming, are examples of other unhealthy ways teens cope with stress.

This list doesn't cover all the positive and negative strategies teens use to cope. Over the years, you may have picked up a strategy or two that doesn't appear here. Feel free to write those in the blank spaces at the end. Place a + sign next to the positive ways you handle stress and a - sign next to the negative ways you handle stress.

Typical Ways Teens Cope with Stress	+/−
I distract myself with schoolwork, gaming, TV, or other activities to get my mind off things.	
I call or hang out with friends for support.	
I use alcohol or drugs to make myself feel better.	
I take a little time to relax, breathe, and unwind.	
I give up trying to deal with it.	
I take action to try to make the situation better.	
I make jokes about the situation.	
I criticize myself.	
I look for something good in what is happening.	
I get involved in a hobby or sport, or in other healthy activities I enjoy.	
I express my negative feelings to people I trust.	
I accept what I can and cannot do and try to live with it.	
I pray or meditate.	
I just ignore the problem and hope it will go away.	
I exercise a little more.	
I eat more than usual.	
I withdraw emotionally and just go through the motions.	
I go shopping to make myself feel good.	
I speak to an adult or teacher I trust about what is stressing me.	
Other:	
Other:	

Take a look at the examples of negative strategies you use to cope. Describe what makes the strategy negative for you.

_____

_____

_____

We often learn strategies for coping by watching friends and parents cope with stress. From whom did you learn the positive strategies you use to cope with stress? What are some examples of this person's positive coping strategies? From whom did you learn the negative strategies you use to cope with stress? What are some examples of this person's negative coping strategies? Noticing whether you're using negative or positive coping strategies is an important step toward changing how you deal with stress.

_____

_____

_____

_____

_____

_____

more to do

After you have thought carefully about the positive and negative ways you cope, answer these questions:

Which of the positive coping strategies are the easiest for you to use and why?

_____

_____

_____

Which of the positive coping strategies work sometimes but not at other times, and why?

_____

_____

_____

3 creating your game plan

for you to know

Feeling overwhelmed, powerless, and out of control signals that you're stressed out—and likely big-time. Making a game plan will help with all these feelings. A game plan breaks things down, identifies a path to follow, and gives you a sense of direction and control over the process of learning to manage your stress.

for you to do

Your days are likely busy. You're probably already running from school to soccer practice to homework, and back to school for a club meeting. Finding time to do something else, even if it's to help you learn to relax and reduce your stress, may be stressing you out. However, you can find time to learn the activities in this workbook and do the other things in your life if you have a game plan. A good game plan identifies when you practice, where you practice, how often you practice, and who you practice with.

When You Practice

In the past, when were the best times for you to learn and practice a new activity? Would those times work now? Was it between school and homework, or first thing in the morning? When are you the freshest during most days? What time of day are you least likely to be interrupted or distracted? Identify a couple of days during the week when you think you could practice the skills in this workbook.

_____

_____

Where You Practice

Where is the quietest and least distracting place to practice? Is there a comfortable place there to sit or to lie down? If a friend asked you for the best place to do homework, where in (or out of) your house would you suggest? Identify a few places to practice that you might want to try first.

_____

_____

How Often You Practice

How often can you practice? Be realistic about the pace of learning. Typically, fifteen to twenty minutes per day is enough. If you can spare only five minutes each day, begin with that and build up to fifteen to twenty minutes. The best practice is the practice you do. It's more important to practice consistently than it is to put in a lot of time inconsistently. Write how often you'll try to practice the workbook activities.

_____

_____

Who You Practice With

Learning and practicing new skills is tough enough, but doing it without support is even tougher. You're more likely to practice the activities in this workbook if you have some support. Who could support you in learning and practicing the activities? Perhaps there's a good friend or family member who could do some things on your to-do list so that you have a little more time to practice. Perhaps you have a friend who is feeling stressed out too, and you could practice the activities together. Write the names of a few people and how they might be able to support you in practicing the workbook activities.

_____

_____

more to do

Learning new skills takes time, patience, and persistence. It's okay to reward yourself for the effort you put into learning the workbook activities. Describe the ways you could reward yourself for each activity you learn and practice. Even small rewards are great (for example, watching your favorite movie again).

_____

_____

_____

_____

keeping a stress diary 4

for you to know

The first step in feeling more relaxed and less stressed is to understand the situations and activities that stress you out and the particular ways you react to stress. A stress diary is a tool that can help you do that.

Jeff knows when he is feeling stressed, but he doesn't always know why. Sometimes he feels so stressed out that he blows up about little things. The other day, his mom asked him to empty the dishwasher and he blew up—it just felt like too much.

Later, when he calmed down, Jeff was able to say, "I'm sorry, Mom"—tearing up a little as he spoke—"I guess I'm just stressed out." Jeff's mom listened and asked him if he knew why, but Jeff couldn't tell her. He just knew that a lot was going on. Junior year was intense and lacrosse practice had started last week, but he had handled that stuff before and it was no sweat. Why was he so stressed out now?

Keeping a stress diary can help you see patterns in your stress. Once you identify the situations and activities that stress you out, you'll know when to use the relaxation and stress reduction skills you'll learn later. Check out Jeff's stress diary and see what he learned.

My Stress Diary	
Date and time:	April 28, 3 p.m.
What happened or what is going on?	My mom asked me to unload the dishwasher.
What was I thinking?	I don't have time for this. I've got too much to do.
How much stress was I feeling (0 to 100, with 0 being none and 100 extreme)?	70
How did my stress make problems for me?	I yelled at my mom, and then I felt really bad about that.
How did I handle my stress this time?	I went to my room and listened to some music to try to chill.
What could I do differently to handle my stress if this happens again?	Maybe take a deep breath before responding?

for you to do

Now you try it. Think of a situation or activity that stresses you out. Use the stress diary to help you see patterns in your stress. Before you start, make several copies of this blank diary (or download a copy at http://www.newharbinger.com/40095) to use later. For as long as you're working on the activities in this book, keep your stress diary. Keeping this diary will help you unpack your stress so that you better understand the pieces of it, and it will help you see the progress you're making as you work through the activities in this workbook.

My Stress Diary	
Date and time:	
What happened or what is going on?	
What was I thinking?	
How much stress was I feeling (0 to 100)?	
How did my stress make problems for me?	
How did I handle my stress this time?	
What could I do differently to handle my stress if this happens again?	

more to do

After you have made a few entries in your stress diary, see if you notice a pattern in your stress. Is there a particular time of day when you're the most stressed (for example, in the morning as you're getting ready for school, in the evening when you're tired or doing homework, at bedtime)?

_____

_____

_____

Are there particular people who stress you out? Are there activities, such as tests or meeting new people, that tend to stress you out?

_____

_____

_____

_____

Do you feel more stressed out when you're doing certain things (for example, soccer practice, homework, math class)?

_____

_____

_____

What are the usual ways that you think about things that might make you feel stressed out (for example, "I'll never get all this done!" "I'm going to fail the history test." "All my teachers hate me.")?

_____

_____

_____

_____

_____

Relaxing Your Stressed-Out Body

5 slow deep breathing

for you to know

We breathe all day long and almost never think about it, but we breathe differently when we're stressed. Stressed breathing is rapid, shallow, and up high in your chest. Relaxed breathing is slow and deep in your abdomen. Relaxed breathing slows your heart rate, soothes your muscles, and brings more oxygen to your body and brain. Slow deep breathing can calm your body quickly and override the tendency to breathe rapidly when you're stressed.

for you to do

Learning slow deep breathing is easy. In just three steps, you can relax when you're feeling stressed:

Step 1: Close your eyes and imagine you have a red balloon attached to the end of a long tube that starts in your nose and ends in your stomach. Place your hand on your stomach over your navel, and feel how that balloon inflates and deflates in rhythm with the rise and fall of your stomach.

Step 2: Keep your hand resting on your stomach, and inhale slowly and deeply through your nose as you count to three. Pause and hold your breath for the count of three, and then slowly exhale through your mouth. Imagine the red balloon inflating as you inhale and deflating as you exhale. Take another slow deep breath in through your nose as you count to three. Hold it for one-two-three, and release for one-two-three. Pause for a moment and inhale, one-two-three. Hold for one-two-three, and exhale for one-two-three. Pause.

Step 3: This time as you inhale, say to yourself the word "calm" and see the word in your mind's eye as you inhale, one-two-three. Hold for one-two-three and say to yourself the word "mind," and see the word in your mind's eye as you exhale one-two-three. Repeat this. Inhale, "calm" one-two-three. Hold one-two-three, and exhale, "mind" one-two-three. Pause.

Practice slow deep breathing for two or three minutes at first and then, over time, increase your practice time until you reach ten to fifteen minutes. If your mind wanders during the activity, just refocus your attention on the picture of the word ("calm" or "mind") in your mind's eye and continue inhaling and exhaling, slowly and deeply.

After you have practiced slow deep breathing several times each day for a couple of days, describe how this activity helped you handle a stressful situation that came up at home or school. What did you notice? Did you feel a bit less stressed? Did you calm down more quickly?

_____

_____

_____

more to do

Now that you've learned about this breathing skill, think about situations in which you could use it to relax. Circle the stressful situations when you want to try the slow deep breathing skill:

Taking an exam

Friends pressuring you to take sides

Going on a date

Hearing your parents argue

Speaking with a teacher

Hanging out at a party

Performing in a recital or game

Doing homework

Taking your driver's test

Arguing with your best friend

Doing something new for the first time

Flying in a plane

In the space below, list events or situations in which you often feel stressed, either from the list above, or any events or situations that don't appear in the list. You can also download a blank copy of the worksheet at http://www.newharbinger.com/40095).

Now select a couple of stressful events or situations that tend to happen repeatedly for you at home or at school. Close your eyes and imagine one of these situations, and rate your stress level on a scale from 0 to 10 (0 being completely relaxed and 10 being highly stressed). Then practice slow deep breathing for five minutes, and rate your stress level *after* your practice.

Tracking My Slow Deep Breathing		
Imagined Stressful Event or Situation	Stress Level *Before* Slow Deep Breathing	Stress Level *After* Slow Deep Breathing

Describe what it was like for you to breathe slowly and deeply as you imagined a stressful event or situation. How quickly did you feel relaxed and calm? What else did you learn that is helpful?

_____

_____

_____

The three steps of slow deep breathing might not have worked like you had hoped. What could you change about the skill that might work better for you next time?

_____

_____

_____

progressive muscle relaxation 6

for you to know

Stress, particularly daily stress, causes your muscles to grow increasingly tense and tight. Progressive muscle relaxation is an activity you can easily learn to relax your body fully. Think of this activity as a daily vitamin for stress. With progressive muscle relaxation, you reset your stress level so that you begin the next day with a calm, relaxed body and feel less stressed by things that come up at school or home.

for you to do

Let's try a progressive muscle relaxation exercise and see what it does to your stress. This activity may be easier for you to learn if you read the following instructions aloud and record them on your phone or another recording device. That way, you can listen to the recording in bed at night to help you practice.

Find a quiet place, and get into a comfortable position. Loosen any tight clothing so that you can breathe easily. Start by squeezing your eyes tight; then scrunch your nose as if you just smelled a rotten egg, pull the edges of your mouth back toward your ears into a forced smile (like you're experiencing g-forces), and bite down to tense your mouth and jaw. Count slowly to fifteen. Then slowly release your eyes, nose, mouth, and jaw for another fifteen seconds. Relax your face so that all the wrinkles disappear and your face is smooth, your cheeks feel soft, and your tongue is loose in your mouth. Notice how different this feels from when your face was tight and tense.

Now move to your neck and shoulders. Tuck your neck into your shoulders like a scared turtle. Hold this position for fifteen seconds, observing the pull on your neck muscles and the discomfort you feel. Now release, and let your shoulders drop down and relax your head. Hold for fifteen seconds.

Next, move to the hands and arms. Make fists with your hands and cross your arms at the wrists. Hold your arms up in front of you and push them together as if you were arm wrestling with yourself. Hold your arms in this position with your fists clenched for fifteen seconds. Then let your fists uncurl and your arms slowly fall to your side. Hold this position for fifteen seconds.

Now suck in your stomach, making your abdomen get hard and tight, and clench your buttock muscles together. Hold this position for fifteen seconds. Notice how the tension feels uncomfortable. Then release and let your stomach go out farther and farther while you release your buttock muscles. Do this for fifteen seconds. As you go through all of these muscle exercises, tensing and relaxing, you might notice that you're starting to feel more relaxed.

Next, tighten your leg muscles by pointing your feet straight out and bending your ankles back toward you. While holding this position, curl your toes into a tight ball. Hold for fifteen seconds, and then release for fifteen seconds. Your legs might feel loose and floppy as they begin to feel relaxed. Repeat these steps to relax your body even more, beginning again with your eyes.

more to do

Though progressive muscle relaxation is one of the most effective strategies you can use to relax your body and increase your ability to handle stress, there are many other strategies you can use. For example, exercise—even just a short walk around the block—is a great stress reducer. Some teens find that taking a hot bath or shower relaxes their bodies, particularly at bedtime when it can help to downshift the mind and body so that sleep comes quickly and easily.

Circle any of these physical activities that you do to reduce your stress:

Hiking with a friend	Jumping rope
Dancing in your room	Bowling
Yoga	Spin training
Swimming	Calisthenics
Rollerblading	Baseball
Jogging	Tennis
Rock climbing	Riding a bike
Dance class	Running in place
Weight lifting	Shooting baskets

Think of physical activities you've never tried or have tried and love but never seem to find time to do. Select one or two of these activities and commit to doing them this week. Write the activities on the lines below and when you plan to do them.

_____

_____

_____

_____

_____

_____

_____

shifting into automatic relaxation 7

for you to know

The best relaxation strategy is one that you can shift into immediately and automatically, particularly when stress hits you quickly and without warning. You've already learned two skills that you'll use to practice automatic relaxation—slow deep breathing and progressive muscle relaxation. Once you learn to shift into automatic relaxation, you'll be able to relax and calm yourself anywhere and at any time in a matter of seconds.

for you to do

The goal of automatic relaxation is to train yourself to bring on the relaxation response with a sign or cue. The relaxation response is a bit like a cat. Your cat might run to you when you're holding a can of cat food and she sees you pulling a can opener out of a drawer. In her mind, the can opener means she should come to you for food. That's the way automatic relaxation works. Signal for relaxation and it comes.

To learn automatic relaxation, you'll use the slow deep breathing and progressive muscle relaxation skills along with an automatic relaxation cue to bring on the relaxation response quickly. Select a cue that you see regularly throughout your day (for example, a ring or sport bracelet you wear regularly, the clock on the wall of math class), and follow these steps:

Step 1: Look at your automatic relaxation cue. Take two or three deep breaths, exhaling slowly through your mouth. Keep your eyes open and focused on the relaxation cue.

Step 2: Each time you exhale, think "calm" or another word or phrase that feels relaxing to you (for example, serenity, cool blue water). Again, keep your eyes open and focused on your cue.

Step 3: With your eyes open and focused on your cue, let the feeling of relaxation spread throughout your body. Scan your body for any tension. Focus on the tense muscles, and empty them of tension.

What muscles seemed to store tension? What did it feel like to let relaxation spread into these muscles?

_____

_____

_____

Practice these steps once a day for three days, using your relaxation cue. If you want to shift into relaxation in several settings, try practicing with several different relaxation cues. For example, at home you can practice with a pattern on your bedroom curtain or rug. At school, you may want to use a relaxation cue that is invisible to everyone but you. Some teens use a ring or friendship bracelet. It doesn't matter what you use as long as it's an object that you see or wear on a daily basis.

more to do

If you've been using your stress diary (from activity 4), you probably have a pretty good idea of when you're feeling stressed and what tends to stress you out. The final step—or more advanced step—is to practice the automatic relaxation activity at the first signs of stress in real life; for example, walking into math class if math stresses you out. Follow these steps as soon as you notice a physical sign of stress (your heart rate increases, your face feels warm):

Step 1: Take two or three slow deep breaths, and look at your relaxation cue. You can close your eyes if you're in a situation where that's okay.

Step 2: Think the relaxing word or phrase as you continue to breathe slowly and deeply. Breathe in and exhale...cool blue water...breathe in and exhale...cool blue water.

Step 3: Scan your body for tension and release the tension as you exhale and think "cool blue water." Also, practice with your eyes open so you feel confident that you can shift into automatic relaxation while doing a stressful eye-open activity, such as taking a math test.

With time and practice, just looking at your relaxation cue and thinking your automatic relaxation phrase, "cool blue water," may be enough to bring on relaxation.

Describe three times you successfully shifted into automatic relaxation. Where were you? What was stressing you out? Where did you feel the tension in your body?

_____

_____

_____

Focusing Your Attention to Relax Your Stressed-Out Mind

8 meditation

for you to know

Meditation is a tool you can use to shift your attention away from the things that stress you or make you anxious. When you practice meditation regularly, you'll become really good at staying calm in general. Also, with a lot of practice, you can learn to shift your attention quickly, sometimes even before you realize it, so that you're calmer in stressful situations.

Wendy's older sister returned home from her first year of college looking and sounding different. She said the first year was super stressful but she had taken a meditation class that had helped a lot. Over dinner, Wendy's sister explained that meditation was becoming very popular. She said, "Tibetan monks aren't the only people meditating these days." She went on to explain that learning to meditate took time and was difficult at first, and that she had started with small periods of practice and increased the time as it became easier.

Wendy didn't say much to her sister, but that night, sitting on her bed, she tried it. She closed her eyes and imagined a big white flower on the magnolia tree outside her bedroom window. Each time her attention drifted to a thought, feeling, or sound, she gently directed it back to the image of the flower. She realized quickly that her sister was right. Meditation was not easy. However, she started with thirty seconds a couple of times that night, and after a few weeks, she was meditating for five minutes and then for ten minutes. After several more weeks, she started to notice that she felt more relaxed during the day and was sleeping better. Also, and this surprised her the most, she was focusing better in her classes. That helped a lot because school was the most stressful situation for her.

for you to do

When you meditate, you learn to focus your attention on an anchor. A meditation anchor can be anything—the movement of your chest as you breathe, a sound in the room, a word you chant aloud or to yourself, or a peaceful and neutral image. When your attention wanders to your thoughts or feelings, the anchor pulls you back to the meditation and to the present moment, just the way an anchor pulls a ship back to the same place when a wave rolls into the harbor.

Coming up with your personal anchor can be fun. Start by practicing with a word as your anchor. Circle the words that feel the most relaxing to you. Write your own personal anchors in the blank lines.

Flower	Mountain	God
Ocean	Water	Home
Peace	Sleep	Friendship
Sunset	Quiet	Calm
Tree	Free	_____
Sky	Clouds	_____
Summer	Love	_____
Moon	Relax	

Select one of the words you circled or wrote to focus on during your first meditation practice. Find a quiet place. Close your eyes and silently repeat the word to yourself. As you repeat the word, visualize a calming image for the word. For example, if the word is moon, visualize a beautiful full moon on a warm and quiet night. Focus your attention on the word and image. Describe how the meditation felt.

_____

_____

_____

Describe what you liked about the meditation.

_____

_____

_____

Describe what you didn't like about the meditation.

_____

_____

_____

more to do

Develop a plan to practice meditation regularly. Would mornings or evenings work best for you? Where is the best place for you to practice? Describe the time and place to meditate that works best for you.

_____

_____

_____

_____

_____

9 mindfulness: five-senses awareness

for you to know

Mindfulness is being aware of yourself, your actions, and your surroundings in the present moment. When you're truly mindful, your mind is clear of what is distracting so that you can tune in to what you're experiencing and doing in the moment. For busy teens, one of the best ways to practice mindfulness is to be mindful while you're doing an activity.

for you to do

You can walk to school in a mindful way if you're aware of the feel of your foot as you place it on the ground and the color of the sky around you. You can eat your lunch mindfully if you pay attention to the feel of the food in your mouth and the taste of the food as you chew it. You can even write your name in a mindful way if you pay attention to the feel of the pencil in your hand and the sound the pencil makes on the paper.

In a mindful activity, you can observe every detail of the experience. It doesn't matter what activity you choose, so long as it's brief, you can do it every day, and it provides opportunities to pay attention to the five senses (sight, smell, taste, touch, sound). For example, to engage your five senses, as you walk from the front door to the kitchen, first focus on the smells of your house. Then, observe the pattern in the carpet or drapes. Feel the weight beneath your feet and the sound you make walking across the carpet or floor. Pay attention to where you place your keys or lunch bag and the sounds they make as you drop them there. At first, you may wish to pay attention to one sense (for example, what you see in the moment), while you do an activity, adding senses (smell, taste, touch, sound) as you get better at the mindful activity.

Circle any of the activities below that you could do using your five senses:

Combing your hair

Washing dishes

Eating a snack or lunch

Applying nail polish

Walking to school or bus

Drinking a glass of water

Washing your face

Vacuuming your room

Tying your shoes

Brushing your teeth

Walking up the stairs

Putting on a shirt

Select some activities, perhaps two or three, from the previous list that you normally rush through, like brushing your teeth, and commit to practicing them in a mindful way. Write the activities on the lines below. Next to the activity, circle the senses that you want to pay attention to. For example, you'll certainly want to pay attention to taste if your mindful activity is eating.

Activity	Senses				
	Sight	Sound	Touch	Taste	Smell
	Sight	Sound	Touch	Taste	Smell
	Sight	Sound	Touch	Taste	Smell
	Sight	Sound	Touch	Taste	Smell

more to do

Doing several things at the same time is the opposite of mindful activity. What things do you tend to do at the same time (for example, listening to music while eating your breakfast, talking on the phone while walking to class)?

_____

_____

_____

Select several activities you do at the same time (eating and reading the newspaper, texting while walking). Now, commit to doing a single activity mindfully (eating only, walking only) every time for one week. What activity did you try to do mindfully? How hard did you find it to do a single activity in a mindful way?

_____

_____

_____

When you were able to be mindful, did you notice a difference in how you felt? Describe the feelings and what you learned.

_____

_____

_____

Was it difficult to be in the present moment? What thoughts and feelings kept taking you away from the activity you were doing mindfully?

_____

_____

_____

10 visualization

for you to know

Our minds are powerful, and one of the most powerful things our minds do is produce images. Some of these images cause us to feel happy, and others cause us to feel anxious or stressed. And once our minds produce an image, our bodies react to that image as if it's real. Conjuring images is called visualization, and visualizing a peaceful scene can create calming moments throughout your day.

James is a decent student, but tests stress him out big time. James started to practice visualization on test days. On those days, he'd arrive five minutes early to class, sit in his seat, and close his eyes. He'd then picture himself floating on a raft in a pool all alone. He felt comfortable and relaxed as the sun warmed his skin. He visualized until the other students and the teacher arrived and then repeated the visualization while the teacher distributed the test booklets. When he opened his eyes and opened the test booklet, he felt calmer and more confident about the test.

for you to do

It's easier to learn to visualize when you're not stressed, so begin to practice visualization when you're relaxed. After some practice, you can try the activity before a stressful event, such as before you present in front of your class at school or before you have a difficult conversation with a friend.

Set aside four to five minutes for this visualization activity. Find a quiet place to sit comfortably, and close your eyes. Take four slow deep breaths, and then imagine a peaceful, calming place. As you imagine the place, permit yourself to look around and notice everything you can see. Notice the colors and the textures of the things around you. Feel the peace and comfort around you. Listen to any sounds present in this peaceful place. All the sounds are pleasing to you and add to the peace and comfort of the setting. Notice any scents in the air that are also pleasing to you. Inhale the pleasing scents and feel the relaxation calm your entire body. Notice now that everything you touch feels good to you. The textures against your skin are comforting and calming. As you experience time in this calm and peaceful place, you're filled with a strong sense of security, serenity, and balance. You feel safe, centered, and grounded.

Sit quietly in this imagined place and feel the peace and calm within you. You'll remember this place and this feeling. Now bring yourself back to the room you're in. As you leave the image, know that you can take yourself back to this peaceful place any time that you wish. The peace is always within you.

Describe what it was like for you to do this activity. Would you change anything about the image or how you did it?

_____

_____

_____

more to do

Think through a typical day, and identify stressful situations that tend to come up for you. Write these stressful situations on the lines below.

_____

_____

_____

For the next few days, practice visualization in these situations. For example, try the visualization activity while you wait for the coach to put you in the game or while you wait your turn to give a presentation to the class. The more you practice visualization in these stressful situations, the more confident you'll feel that you can quickly relax in situations that tend to stress you out.

Working Your Way Through Worry

11 your sources of worry

for you to know

If you ask people why they feel worried, they'll often tell you about the situation they're in: "I'm worried because I have a test tomorrow." Or, "I'm worried because I'm going to ask someone out." While the situation is important, your thoughts play a major role in your emotions. Identifying the types of anxious thoughts you tend to have is the first step in learning to manage your worry.

for you to do

Different teens often have very different thoughts about the same situation. Imagine two teens who have a history test next week. The first teen thinks, "History is a tough subject for me but I have the time to prepare, so it will be okay." This teen's worry motivates her to study for the exam and ask her teacher for help. The second teen thinks, "I'm an idiot when it comes to history. I'm going to flunk that test for sure." This teen's worry is extreme, and he puts off studying and thinks there isn't any point in asking his teacher for help. As you can see, our thoughts directly influence our feelings and actions.

Next are common situations in which teens have worry thoughts. For each category, describe the situation that triggered this particular worry thought, and describe the specific thought itself, using the words that actually went through your mind when you were in the situation. For further practice, download the worksheet My Sources of Worry at http://www.newharbinger.com/40095.

My Sources of Worry	
Performance (tests, athletics, dating)	
Situation	Worry Thought
Siting on the bench halfway through my basketball game.	If I don't get any playing time, everyone will think I'm no good.
Friends	
Situation	Worry Thought
Texted a friend an hour ago, and I haven't heard back.	She always has her phone on her. She must be mad at me.

Family	
Situation	Worry Thought
Asked my parents if I can go to a concert and they said they'll think about it.	They won't let me go. My friends will have fun without me, and I'll be left out of the group next time.

Health	
Situation	Worry Thought
Feeling stomach discomfort.	Oh no, I'm getting sick. I can't get sick right now. I have too much to do, and if I miss any more school I won't be able to catch up.

World Events (environmental, political)	
Situation	Worry Thought
Reading a news story about climate change.	Things are just getting worse and worse. No one seems to care about this at all. My parents are doing nothing, and my friends aren't thinking about it.

Other Types of Worry Thoughts (being late, plane crashing)	
Situation	Worry Thought

more to do

Let's try to understand our worry thoughts even better. Worry thoughts tend to spin around a bigger fear, and this fear may be driving your worry. For example, if you worry a lot about failing tests, the bigger fear may be that your friends will think you're a loser and won't hang out with you anymore. For each worry thought, starting with the one that comes up most often, ask yourself two questions: (1) If the thing you worry about happened, what would be so bad about that? (2) What will happen if that fear comes true?

For example, if you worry about failing a test: (1) I'll get a really bad grade in the class and then won't get into the college I want to go to. (2) My friends will think I'm lazy or stupid and won't want to hang out with me anymore.

Now it's your turn. If the thing you worry about happened, what would be so bad about that?

_____

_____

_____

What will happen if that fear comes true? When answering this question, remember that often our fears don't come true. If the unlikely event does happen, teens usually fear it will be worse than it actually is. You likely have successfully handled things going wrong before. When you answer this question, try to be realistic. Think about how you can best manage the fear coming true and who might help you handle it.

_____

_____

_____

your thinking mistakes 12

for you to know

Certain kinds of thoughts spark worry, and when these thoughts get going, they can take over your thinking. These worry thoughts tend to overestimate the likelihood of something bad happening when it's not likely at all or, if it does happen, to overestimate how horrible it would be. These types of unhelpful thoughts are called thinking mistakes. Every person on the planet makes thinking mistakes sometimes. Catching the mistakes when they shoot through your mind can help you manage your stress and anxiety.

for you to do

There are many different types of thinking mistakes. This activity focuses on three that anxious teens tend to make. When you learn to catch a thinking mistake while it's happening, it becomes much easier to calm yourself and do what you want to do.

Thinking Mistake 1: Jumping to Conclusions

When you feel anxious, your mind starts to jump to conclusions about what is going to happen. Since you're anxious, it's likely those conclusions are pretty scary. For example, you'd be jumping to conclusions if you conclude that a friend who didn't respond to a text message within the first thirty minutes doesn't like you.

Thinking Mistake 2: Tunnel Vision

When you feel anxious, you may see only the worst. You don't see anything that would contradict the worst. It's like you're looking down a tunnel and all you see is bad news. For example, if the other team scores three goals against you in your first game as goalie on varsity soccer, then you might start to look through the tunnel. You might think only about the three goals the other team scored and not see the many other shots you blocked.

Thinking Mistake 3: Mind Reading

When you feel anxious, you may believe that you know what someone else is thinking. This is mind reading. You assume that your teammates think you're a terrible shortstop because you made an error in the last inning.

Now test yourself. Decide which of these examples are thinking mistakes and then write the type of mistake:

Thought: *I spent a week studying for the chemistry test. There is no way I'm prepared enough. I'm going to flunk that test big time.*

Is it a thinking mistake?   Yes   No

If yes, what type? _____

Thought: *Chemistry is my worst subject. My teacher must think I'm the dumbest student in the class.*

Is it a thinking mistake?   Yes   No

If yes, what type? _____

Thought: *I have a C+ in math. I don't know anything about math.*

Is it a thinking mistake?   Yes   No

If yes, what type? _____

Answer key: 1) Yes; jumping to conclusions. 2) Yes; mind reading. 3) Yes; tunnel vision.

more to do

Take some time to catch thinking mistakes throughout your day. Look for situations in which you feel worried and anxious. Notice your worry thoughts and decide whether any of them are thinking mistakes. Write down the thought and the thinking mistake (and download the worksheet Catching My Thinking Mistakes at http:// www.newharbinger.com/40095 for further practice).

_____

_____

_____

As you read or watch a movie, notice any characters who tend to make thinking mistakes. Write down the character, the thought, and the thinking mistake.

_____

_____

_____

13 the key question: where's the evidence?

for you to know

Looking for thinking mistakes is very helpful. Once you catch those mistakes, what do you do next? Well, you step back and focus on a more accurate, helpful view of the situation that has you worried. To do that, ask yourself the key question: where's the evidence? Finding the evidence will help you shrink stress by challenging your worry thoughts, rather than assuming they're true. Once you have all the facts, worry thoughts lose some of their power.

for you to do

Jordan is a good student and a bit of a science wonk. He decided to take a gap year before college to work for his uncle who is a biologist. While Jordan knows that a gap year is a good decision for him, he's worrying nonstop that his friends will think he's a loser for not going straight to college. After two weeks of worry, Jordan realizes that he's mind reading. He really doesn't know what his friends are thinking about his decision or about him. Jordan decides to apply a little science to the problem. He asks himself the key question: where's the evidence? Then he writes down the evidence in a table like the following:

Thought: My friends will think I'm a loser and too immature for college when I tell them I'm taking a gap year.

Evidence That the Thought Is True	Evidence That the Thought Isn't True
1. My five close friends are all going to college right away. 2. My brother went to college right away, and so did my cousins.	1. My friends have always been okay with my decisions. They've never judged me before. 2. Doing what is best for me is a sign of maturity, not of being a loser. 3. Two other students in my class are taking a gap year. 4. My friends might not know what I'm doing with my gap year, and if they did, they might think it's a great idea too.

New Thought: Although I don't know how my friends will react to my decision, there is plenty of evidence that they'll be okay with it, especially when I tell them what I'm doing in my gap year.

Now you try. Choose a worry that is bugging you. Ask yourself the key question: where's the evidence? List the evidence that the thought is true and the evidence that the thought isn't true. Next, write a new thought line, summarizing the evidence as a statement that is more accurate and helpful about the situation.

Finding the Evidence	
Thought:	
Evidence That the Thought Is True	Evidence That the Thought Isn't True
New thought:	

For further practice, you can download the worksheet Finding the Evidence at http://www.newharbinger.com/40095.

more to do

At first, it might be difficult for you to find evidence that a worry thought isn't true. Keep at it, though. It's there. There are many ways to collect evidence. You can search the web or take a poll of your friends. Be creative. For example, Jordan could check websites to find the number of students in his high school, or even in his state, who take a gap year. Write down one experiment you could do to gather more evidence about the worry thought.

_____

_____

_____

14 overthrowing the tyranny of "should"

for you to know

You may tell yourself a hundred times a day that you "should" do something. When you do something just because you think you "should," you haven't really made a choice. In fact, doing something just because you think you "should" robs you of choice and adds to your stress, anxiety, and guilt. Without choice, you're a servant to the "should" tyrant. With choice, you're in charge of your own life and therefore will feel less stressed, anxious, and guilty.

Carlos has studied all night. As he starts to nod off, he thinks, "I should put in another hour but I'm so tired," and then feels guilty for not studying more. When he reads through a difficult problem during his math test, he thinks, "I should know how to do this problem," and feels anxious. After Carlos chatted with Gwynn for a few minutes, he thinks, "I should have talked less to Gwynn and let her do more talking. That was lame," and he feels anxious and guilty.

for you to do

Make a list of the "shoulds" that tend to run through your head and cause you to feel stressed, anxious, or guilty. These thoughts are likely about the kind of friend, student, athlete, or son or daughter you believe you "should" be. Next to each "should," write what will happen or will not happen if you do or don't do the thing you're telling yourself you should do. Is what you gain or lose that important to you? Rate them on a scale from 0 to 10, with 10 being extremely important. For further practice, you can download this worksheet at http://www.newharbinger.com/40095.

Overthrowing the Tyranny of "Should"			
The "should"	What do you lose if you do the thing you "should"?	What do you gain if you don't do the thing you "should"?	How important is it (0–10)?
I should study for the test I'm taking in two weeks, but I'm so tired.	Sleep! I'm so tired in my classes that I'm certain I'm missing important stuff.	More sleep and less stress. I might be able to study less if I'm fully alert and awake in my classes.	10. It's really important to me to do well in school and be awake and alert in my classes.
I should have let Gwynn do more of the talking.	Gwynn won't get to know me if I don't talk, and I want her to get to know me.	I feel less stressed, and the conversation will be easier. That will make Gwynn more comfortable, which is what I want.	8. It's really important to me that Gwynn like me and feel comfortable with me.

The "should"	What do you lose if you do the thing you "should"?	What do you gain if you don't do the thing you "should"?	How important is it (0–10)?

more to do

Go back to the "shoulds" you listed in the previous section. Which "should" statements make you feel the most stressed, anxious, or guilty, and why?

_____

_____

_____

Think through how important it is to you to do something *just* because the "should" tyrant tells you to do it. Do you follow the command of the "should" tyrant who tells you to do something that's not important—say a 2 or 3 on the importance scale? Do you follow the command when it's an 8 on the importance scale? It's up to you to decide what to do or not do, not the "should" tyrant.

15 following the path of value

for you to know

In the previous activity, you learned that you have a choice about what to do or not do. Perhaps you've been following "shoulds" because you truly believed they motivated you. Now that you've learned otherwise, you might wonder what actually does motivate you. The answer is your core values, which separate what you think you "should" do from what you wish to do, which is bigger and more important than the long list of "shoulds." To live a fuller, less stressful life, it's time to follow your core values.

for you to do

Think back to the last scene of *The Wizard of Oz*. Dorothy and her friends, Lion, Scarecrow, and Tin Man, stand next to her. As they say goodbye to each other, the wizard honors their unique core values. For the Lion, it's courage. For the Scarecrow, it's intelligence. For the Tin Man, it's love, and for Dorothy, it's family or home. Imagine that you're standing there too. Which of your core values would the wizard honor? Is friendship one of your core values? If yes, this might explain how much time and effort you're willing to put into making your friendships caring and supportive. Is creativity one of your core values? If yes, this might explain your passion for drawing or music. Is it achievement? If yes, this might explain your willingness to practice your free throw shots over and over. In the table below, place a check next to the five core values that are most important to you. Feel free to add other core values to the list.

Core Value	✓
Adventure	
Belonging	
Creativity	
Determination	
Excellence	
Family	
Generosity	
Helping	
Intelligence	
Justice	
Loyalty	
Making a difference	

Core Value	✓
Originality	
Patriotism	
Quality	
Reliability	
Self-reliance	
Spirituality	
Teamwork	
Uniqueness	
Vitality	
Other:	
Other:	
Other:	

more to do

Go back to the previous activity and look at your list of "shoulds." These are the "shoulds" that add stress, anxiety, and guilt to your days. Now, reword each "should" as a choice to pursue a core value. For example, for the statement "I should be a better student," you could write: "I choose to work hard in school because learning about the world and myself are important to me." For the statement "I should be more patient with my friends," you could write: "I choose to work hard to understand where my friends are coming from, because when I do this, my friends feel like I care, which makes my friendships stronger and this is important to me."

_____

_____

_____

_____

_____

On the line below, select one core-value statement to practice as a first step following your own path of value.

_____

_____

_____

Working Your Way Through Fear

16 building a plan to work your way through fear

for you to know

Anxiety and avoidance go together like peanut butter and jelly. You'll avoid, if possible, anything that frightens you. Avoiding dangerous things makes sense. If you're hiking and see a grizzly bear ahead, it's smart to go the other way; grizzly bears are truly dangerous. However, tests and friendships aren't grizzly bears. Avoiding them not only doesn't make sense but can make your life more difficult. When you repeatedly avoid things that make you anxious, your life becomes smaller and more stressful.

for you to do

The more often we face a fear, the less fear we feel. Think back to a time when you were afraid to do something you had not done before. Perhaps it was your first big soccer game or recital. Perhaps it was your first stay at sleepaway camp. How afraid did you feel before the first game? And after the second game? How afraid did you feel the first time you slept away from home? What about the third time you slept away from home? Yes, the more often we face a fear, the less fear we feel. It's the way fear works.

Charlotte was afraid of making a mistake in front of people. She decided to come up with a list of situations that made her nervous. Charlotte's list looked like this:

Answering a question in class

Telling a story to a group of people

Sharing her writing for peer review in English class

Playing guitar in front of other people

Asking someone to go to a movie

In the tables that follow, place a check next to the situations that make you anxious and that you tend to avoid, and add your own too:

Avoidance of Social Situations	✓
Talking in a group	
Talking on the phone	
Initiating a social get-together	
Attending social activities (parties, group dinners, dances) Activity _____ Activity _____ Activity _____	
Talking to adults	
Talking to new people	
Other:	

Avoidance at School	✓
Asking or answering questions in class	
Asking the teacher a question one-on-one	
Giving a report or presentation in class	
Taking a test	
Reading out loud	
Other:	

Avoidance of Other Situations	✓
Public bathrooms	
Elevators	
Telling your parents when something bad has happened	
Being stressed in front of others	
Doing things that you're not good at in front of others	
Other:	

more to do

Psychologists have a name for shrinking your fears by facing them repeatedly: it's called *exposure*. Since exposure means approaching the things you fear, it can feel intimidating. It's easy to convince yourself that avoiding things isn't a big deal, or that your fears will go away on their own one day. Unfortunately, that's not how fear works. Avoiding a fear keeps it going. For example, if you're afraid to make a mistake and avoid raising your hand in class to answer the teacher's question, your fear will never get any better. Facing the fear helps you learn that making a mistake is no big deal. However, avoiding raising your hand and taking a small chance means you never learn that there isn't anything to fear.

In the next two activities, you'll learn how to face your fear (exposure) to shrink it. Because exposure is scary, it helps to spend some time thinking through the pluses of facing your fears. Write the good things that will happen when you begin to avoid things less often. Perhaps you'll make more friends or feel less stressed all day long. Perhaps you'll sleep better or feel more confident.

_____

_____

_____

_____

_____

17 building your act-brave ladder

for you to know

The next step in overcoming your fears is to build an act-brave ladder. An act-brave ladder is a list of situations in which you can practice acting brave. Your act-brave ladder is the road map you'll follow to overcome your fear. It has a first step and a last step and steps in between, and with each step, you'll grow more confident and less fearful.

Adolfo avoided talking in a group, asking a friend to hang out, or giving presentations, because he was afraid that he would say something stupid or weird. Adolfo wanted to overcome this fear, but he didn't feel confident that he could present to a big group of kids he didn't know well. That was too scary. One day, Adolfo listened to his soccer coach explain the steps that go into a good free kick. His coach broke it down, and then Adolfo and his teammates practiced each step over and over. This way of practicing made sense to him. Break it down, his coach reminded the team. It occurred to Adolfo that he could break down his plan to overcome his fear of speaking to people too.

for you to do

If Adolfo asked for your help working on his fear of giving presentations, how would you help him? Would you sign him up for the talent show in front of the whole school or start small and ask him to give a short presentation to just you? Yes, starting with small fears and working toward the bigger fears is the best way to overcome a fear. Look at the act-brave ladder Adolfo built to overcome his fear of giving presentations.

Giving a Presentation	Anxiety Level (0–10)
Participate in a school play or talent show.	10
Give a presentation in English class.	7
Practice presentations for a friend.	5

Did you notice how Adolfo rated his anxiety level for each step on his ladder? He imagined how nervous he would feel if he practiced the step (from 0 to 10, where 0 is completely relaxed and 10 is extremely anxious). Adolfo doesn't have any steps below a 5-anxiety level. There's not much wiggle room in Adolfo's act-brave ladder. That can make it tough for him to get started and to be successful. Can you think of three easier steps that Adolfo could add to his act-brave ladder? Write them in the following table.

Giving a Presentation	Anxiety Level (0–10)
Participate in a school play or talent show.	10
Give a presentation in English class.	7
Practice presentations for a friend.	5

Now, make several copies of the act-brave ladder (or download the worksheet at http://www.newharbinger.com/40095). Select one of your fears and create an act-brave ladder for it. Break it down into steps like Adolfo did. What details of the situation might make it harder or easier? Be creative. If you end up with too many high-anxiety items, look for ways to break those steps down into smaller and less scary steps.

My Act-Brave Ladder	
I want to overcome my fear of:	Anxiety Level (0–10)
Step 1.	
Step 2.	
Step 3.	
Step 4.	
Step 5.	
Step 6.	

more to do

Now that you have the idea, think of other fears you have, and create ladders for them too. Remember, if you're avoiding a situation, activity, or thing, you're likely afraid of it. Working your way through those fears with an act-brave ladder can help, no matter what the fear is. In the next activity, you'll use your act-brave ladder to learn the best ways to practice facing your fears.

putting your working-your-way-through-fear plan to the test 18

for you to know

Our brains and bodies often do everything they can to get away from fear. You might tell yourself that you'll face your fear tomorrow or decide that doing what you're afraid to do isn't that important. Perhaps you start out facing the fear, but over time, you begin to practice less often, although you know it helps. Overcoming a fear is a marathon, not a sprint, and a practice plan can help you stay on track and succeed.

for you to do

Select one of the act-brave ladders you created in activity 17. Decide how often, where, and when you'll practice the first few steps on the ladder. The more you practice, the better. For example, if you were afraid of speaking in class, do you think raising your hand in math class once a semester would be enough to overcome your fear of speaking? What about once a month? What about once a day? Like most things, the more you practice, the better you get. Look at Jason's practice plan for speaking in class:

Act-brave ladder: Talking in class

How often I'll practice: Once each day, five days each week

Day	Challenge	Anxiety level (0–10)	What did you predict would happen?	What actually happened?
Monday	Raise hand in math during private work time	5	People around me will think my question was stupid.	No one seemed to notice or react to my question.
Tuesday	Answer a question in English class that I'm confident of	5	I'll get the question wrong and look like I don't know anything.	I got the question right and the class continued.
Wednesday	Answer a question in English class when I'm unsure of the answer	6	I'll get the question wrong and look like I don't know anything.	I got it wrong. The person who answered after me got it wrong too. It didn't look like anyone noticed or was upset about this.

It's important to make certain that you're learning something important from all your hard work. Notice the far-right column, in which Jason wrote what actually happened. This is an important step. Paying attention to the accuracy or inaccuracy of the predictions that make you anxious will help you learn that you have nothing to fear.

Now build your own practice plan. Before each practice, write the prediction that makes you anxious and after each practice, write what really happened.

Act-brave ladder I'm working on: _____

How often I'll practice: _____

Day	Challenge	Anxiety level (0–10)	What did you predict would happen?	What actually happened?

more to do

Sometimes it's difficult to practice overcoming fears on your own. You may want to consider seeking support from the right person. On the lines below, write the names of family members or friends who can encourage you to practice and support you as you work to overcome your fears.

_____

_____

_____

_____

_____

imagining your way through fear 19

for you to know

Our imaginations are very powerful. Using your imagination to face your fears is great as a warm-up to a real-life exposure that is too scary to try or when you cannot face the fear in real life because it doesn't occur very often, such as flying on an airplane. By practicing in your imagination, you get used to the worry thoughts, emotions, and physical sensations that will be there when you face the real-life situation.

for you to do

Hannah's classmates selected her to give a speech at their high school graduation, and she was very nervous about it. To prepare, Hannah decided to imagine her way through her fear. She loved books, and she decided to write a short story about giving the graduation speech. It was going to be a scary story, and she included all the things about the speech that she feared, particularly how her body was feeling and what was going through her mind:

I'm sitting on stage waiting to give my speech, and I'm so nervous. I hear the principal call my name. I feel a rush of terror. My heart is beating very fast, and I'm sweating and feel a little sick to my stomach. I walk to the podium, and everyone is staring at me. I want to run off the stage but I can't. All I can think is that everyone sees that I'm a nervous wreck. They'll think my speech is lame and that I'm not that smart. I feel more embarrassed than I've ever felt in my life. I start to speak and my voice...my voice is trembling. The shakiness in my voice is so obvious. I sound stupid. I should have never done this. As I'm talking, people are just staring at me. I just keep going with the speech thinking to myself, "I'll never live this down. I'm incredibly embarrassed. I can't stand it."

Look over your fear ladders and identify any fears that either you cannot practice regularly or that seem too scary to try in real life. Now, take the feared situation and write a short story, just like Hannah did. You want your audience (which is you) to get their money's worth and really feel afraid. Include in the script not only what's going on around you (sounds, smells, things you see), but also what is going on inside your mind (thoughts and images) and inside your body (sweating, shaking). Remember, the goal is to write a script that scares you so that you can practice facing this fear.

_____

_____

_____

_____

_____

_____

more to do

Now that you've written the scary story, close your eyes and imagine it happening. You can read it off the page, or record yourself reading it out loud. Try for a story that is just a few minutes long, but a powerful few minutes. Listen or read the story repeatedly for about fifteen minutes. Practice two or three times a week, or more if you can. The more you practice, the sooner you'll feel calmer with the scene. If you notice that you're spacing out or thinking about something else, gently refocus your attention on the story. While it may seem strange that you're practicing an activity that increases your anxiety in a book focused on reducing your anxiety and stress, remember that by facing your fears in the short run, you'll have much less anxiety and stress in the long run.

Solving the Problems in Your Life So That You Don't Stress About Them

20 identifying the problem (and that's not always easy)

for you to know

One of the most stressful problems is a problem that you don't know how to solve. It just sits there in the back of your mind, spinning and spinning, yet every problem has a solution that can make things a little better for you. The first, and the most important, step in learning to solve a problem that stresses you out is to define the problem in such a way that there is a chance you can solve it.

for you to do

Begin by listing the problems that are stressing you out now. Remember to write the problem in a way that puts solving it in your court—and frames it in such a way that there is some chance that you can solve it. For example, you might not have much control over whether your parents argue. However, you do have some control over what you do when they argue. Do you ask them to argue less? Do you go to a friend's house when they argue? Do you go to your room and listen to music until they stop arguing? Look at the examples below for ideas.

Problem	Problem Defined So That You Can Solve It
I feel very anxious when my parents argue with each other.	I don't know what to do when my parents argue with each other.
I feel totally stressed when my friends ask me to do things I don't want to do.	I don't know how to say no to my friends or to explain why I'm uncomfortable when they ask me to do certain things.
I'm overwhelmed by all the things I have to do.	I'm procrastinating and now I'm terrified that I won't finish my homework.

more to do

Sometimes a problem is so complicated that it's difficult to solve it on your own. In those cases, part of your problem-solving plan could include finding someone to help you. Describe a situation that is stressing you out now. Who could you ask to help you solve it? Why is this person a good choice? Has he or she helped you solve problems in the past? How?

_____

_____

_____

_____

_____

for you to know

After you identify the problem in a way that puts you in control of a solution, the next step is to brainstorm possible solutions while keeping an open mind. Brainstorming can be difficult, particularly when you're feeling overwhelmed and stressed out. Stress tends to shut down brainstorming, which means that you're stuck. No brainstorming, no possible solution.

Anjaylia is stressed out. Her mom has been nagging her to clean her room for days, and she finally said that unless Anjaylia cleans the room tonight she'll ground her for the weekend. Still Anjaylia cannot imagine when she'll do it. She knows it will take only thirty or forty minutes but she has tutoring, a ballet class, and then all her homework. She wants to hang out with her friends after school for a while too. She's overwhelmed and doesn't know what to do.

for you to do

Sometimes the hardest part of brainstorming is to keep an open mind. When you're stressed, you may eliminate a possible solution too quickly because it seems silly or you assume it cannot work. Sometimes a silly solution is the only one that will work. This activity helps you get all the possible solutions on the table so that you can examine them carefully (that's the next activity). Take a look at Anjaylia's brainstorming worksheet.

Problem	Possible Solutions
I can't find time to clean my room tonight.	Ask my sister to help me clean my room tonight.
	Cancel my tutoring appointment and ballet class, and clean my room tonight.
	Do ten minutes of cleaning when I get home from school, ten minutes before dinner, and ten minutes before bed. That's thirty minutes.
	Ask my brother to clean my room tonight. He has plenty of time. Maybe he would do me a favor.

Now look at the list of possible solutions Anjaylia wrote in her brainstorming form. What possible solutions would you add to Anjaylia's list?

_____

_____

_____

What silly solutions would you add?

_____

_____

_____

more to do

Now you try. Describe a problem that is stressing you out and write it in the brainstorming worksheet below (or download a blank copy of the worksheet at http://www.newharbinger.com/40095 and use that). You may want to review activity 20 to make certain you describe the problem in such a way that there is some chance you can solve it. Remember, you may not be able to solve certain problems, like a teacher who gives you too much homework, but you can solve the problem of how you react to the homework problem or how you approach it. There are many activities in this workbook that can help with that. Next, write all possible solutions that come to mind. Remember, effective brainstorming depends on an open mind, so don't eliminate a possible solution too quickly.

My Brainstorming Worksheet	
Problem	Possible Solutions

What was brainstorming like for you? Describe what made this activity easy and difficult for you.

_____

_____

_____

List other problems that are stressing you out for which you think there is no solution. How might brainstorming possible solutions to these problems help you feel less overwhelmed and stressed?

_____

_____

_____

for you to know

Once you identify the problem (see activity 20) and list all possible solutions (see activity 21), no matter how silly the solution or how unlikely it is to work, it's time to look at the pluses and minuses of each solution. Thinking through each possible solution in this way will help you choose a solution that is likely to help, at least a little, and a little help is better than no help at all.

for you to do

No solution is perfect. There are pluses and minuses for every solution. The trick is to find a solution that is likely to work *and* not create more problems for you. Take a look at the pluses and minuses Anjaylia listed for each possible solution to her problem: *I can't find time to clean my room tonight.* How did she do?

Problem I can't find time to clean my room tonight.		
Possible Solutions	**Pluses**	**Minuses**
Ask my sister to help me clean my room tonight.	If my sister helped, I could clean my room in ten minutes, and have time to do other stuff.	My sister and I don't get along, and asking her may stress me out more.
Cancel my tutoring appointment and ballet class, and clean my room tonight.	I would definitely have enough time to do my homework and clean my room.	I love ballet, and it's a great stress reducer. Canceling my tutoring appointment is the last thing I want to do. That would totally freak me out.
Do ten minutes of cleaning when I get home from school, ten minutes before dinner, and ten minutes before bed.	This might work. I think if I really focus, I can clean my room in thirty minutes.	It's still thirty minutes to fit into everything else I'm doing. Maybe thirty minutes won't be enough time.
Ask my brother to clean my room tonight. He has plenty of time. Maybe he would do me a favor.	Well, he does have plenty of time.	This is too funny. My brother's room is a disaster. I'm going to ask him for help? Who am I kidding?

Now, look at the pluses and minuses Anjaylia came up with for all possible solutions. What additional pluses and minuses for the possible solutions would you add to Anjaylia's list?

_____

_____

_____

In looking at possible solutions, which one do you think would create the most problems for her? Which solution would you recommend Anjaylia try?

_____

_____

_____

more to do

Now you try. Describe a problem and then brainstorm all possible solutions. Remember to keep an open mind no matter how silly or impractical the solution. Then write all the pluses and minuses you can think of next to each possible solution. You can ask a close friend or family member for their take on the pluses and minuses for the possible solutions. Sometimes another person will see something important that you missed.

My Problem-Solving Worksheet		
Problem		
Possible Solutions	Pluses	Minuses

The final step is to select the best solution and try it. Remember, the best solution is the one that is most likely to work *and* the least likely to make things worse. Write the best solution on the lines below.

_____

_____

_____

It's always good to have a second-best solution, just in case the best solution doesn't work. This is your backup solution. Write the second-best solution on the lines below.

_____

_____

_____

That's it. Three activities and three steps to solve problems. Try it a few times (perhaps using the My Problem-Solving Worksheet that you can find at http://www .newharbinger.com/40095). With practice, you'll learn that solving problems rather than just worrying about them can decrease your anxiety and stress pretty quickly.

23 the power of constructive worry

for you to know

Worry motivates us to think through a problem and develop a solution for it. This is great, except when you lie awake in bed thinking through an endless string of solutions. Often, worry hits at night because bedtime is the first time things have slowed down enough that your brain has time to solve the day's problems. If you have trouble sleeping because of this kind of unfinished business, constructive worry can help sleep come more quickly.

for you to do

Before you begin this activity, make several copies of the worksheet The Power of Constructive Worry (or download a blank copy at http://www.newharbinger. com/40095) to use in the future when you begin to worry at night. Here are the steps to harnessing the power of constructive worry:

Step 1: Several hours before bed, when you're rested and clearheaded, list in the Concerns column all the concerns that might keep you awake at night.

Step 2: For each concern, write in the Solutions column the first step you might take to solve the problem. This may not be the final solution to the problem, because you solve most problems in steps anyway, so just write your best guess for the first step. If you know how to solve the problem completely, write that solution (for example, "I'll speak to Mr. Samuel about whether I can get some extra credit to bring my grade up."). If you decide that the concern isn't really a big problem and that you'll just deal with it when the time comes, then write that (for example, "I'll wait to see my progress report next week before I speak to Mr. Samuel."). If you decide you just don't know what to do about the problem and will ask someone to help you, write that (for example, "I'll ask Janie if she is doing anything to bring up her grade in Mr. Samuel's class."). Last, if you decide that it's a problem but there isn't a good solution at all, and that you'll just have to live with it, write that down. Add a note to remind you that sometime soon you or someone you know will give you a clue that will lead to a solution (for example, "There isn't any solution to this problem. I bet I'll learn something tomorrow or the next day that could solve the problem, but in the meantime, I'll just live with it.").

The Power of Constructive Worry	
Date and time:	
Concern:	Solutions:

Step 3: Fold the worksheet in half and set it on the nightstand next to your bed. Tell yourself to forget about it until bedtime.

Step 4: At bedtime, if you begin to worry, tell yourself that you have dealt with your unfinished business already in the best way you know how, and you dealt with it when you were rested and at your problem-solving best. Remind yourself that you'll work on the concerns again tomorrow and that nothing you can do when you're tired can help you any more than what you've already done when you were well rested. In fact, more work on the problem will only make matters worse.

more to do

Now that you know how to harness the power of constructive worry, list the typical problems that come up for you at bedtime.

_____

_____

_____

After you have practiced this activity for a couple of nights, describe what this was like for you. How difficult was it to resist worrying?

_____

_____

_____

Worry is helpful, except when it's not. You can harness the power of constructive worry to decrease your stress and sleep better.

Communicating Clearly and Saying No

24 clear communication begins with good listening

for you to know

Clear communication begins with good listening. When you know how to listen, truly listen, you can prevent misunderstandings and, more importantly, work through them effectively. Furthermore, good listening builds strong connections to people. The more solid the connections to friends and family members, the less likely that misunderstandings, which are unavoidable, will damage the relationships with the important people in your life. Strong connections make life easier and less stressful.

for you to do

Place a check next to the characteristics you think make good listeners. Also, add any other characteristics of good listeners that come to mind.

	✓		✓
They make eye contact.		They show interest by nodding their heads and smiling at appropriate times.	
They ask questions to show that they're willing to share the stage.		They ask questions if anything is unclear to them.	
They often check whether they understood the other person: "Do you mean that...?"		They let the other person finish his or her thoughts without interrupting.	
They summarize key points to show that they're listening.		They communicate that they're open to being wrong: "I could be wrong about this but I think..."	
They let go of a topic if the conversation has moved on to something else.		They share their thoughts and likes to keep the conversation going.	
Other:		Other:	
Other:		Other:	

Think of someone who is a good listener. How many of the things in the checklist does that person do?

_____

_____

Think about a time when you were a good listener. What did you do to show the person that you were listening?

_____

_____

_____

How did the person react to your good listening skills?

_____

more to do

Like most things, it takes practice to become a good listener. A good way to practice listening is with a close friend. The next time you're hanging out together, ask your friend a question, then practice good listening. Look at the previous list of good listening characteristics. Place a check next to each good listening skill you used.

Did you listen well?   Yes   No

If yes, which good listening skills did you use?

_____

_____

If no, what did you do that showed you were not listening well?

_____

_____

If there was a misunderstanding, which good listening skill did you use to get the conversation back on track?

_____

_____

25 clear communication includes I-messages

for you to know

Using *I-messages* instead of you-messages is an important way to communicate effectively. I-messages express that you're open to listening. You-messages express that you're not. I-messages put people at ease because what you're saying sounds as if it's about you and not about them, even when it sometimes is about them. Using I-messages improves your relationships with friends, family, and teachers, and better relationships mean less stress in your life.

for you to do

You-messages put people on the defensive because they often include the words "should," "must," "ought to," "need to," "always," and "never." When you say to a friend, "You should try this kind of soda," it sounds as if you're telling him that he's stupid for liking the soda he likes. When you tell a friend, "You never listen to me," it sounds as if you're attacking her.

An I-message includes three parts: I feel…when you…because… Here are a couple of examples:

You're angry with your friend Tina because she's been sitting on the bus with Amy all week and not speaking to you.

You-message: "You never sit and talk with me anymore."

I-message: "I feel hurt when you sit with Amy on the bus and ignore me because it makes me think you don't want to be my friend anymore."

You're angry with your friend Ricardo because he shared his lunch with Tim and didn't offer you any.

You-message: "You should give your lunch to me because I'm your best friend, not Tim."

I-message: "I feel angry when you share your lunch with Tim without asking me if I want some because I think that you like Tim more than me."

For each situation, describe how you would respond with a you-message. Next, change the you-message to an I-message.

A friend doesn't respond to your text messages for an entire day.

You-message: You _____

_____.

I-message: I feel _____ when you _____

because _____.

During your group project, one of the other students keeps interrupting you.

You-message: You _____

_____.

I-message: I feel _____ when you _____

because _____.

The person behind you in class is kicking your chair nonstop.

You-message: You _____

_____.

I-message: I feel _____ when you _____

because _____.

more to do

It takes practice to change you-messages to I-messages because you-messages tend to be automatic. In order to change an automatic response, the first step is to know when you've fallen into the automatic pattern. Tracking can help. Make several copies of the form below to do this activity (or download the My You-Message Diary that you can find at http://www.newharbinger.com/40095). For a couple of weeks, track your you-messages. Describe the situation (who was there and what happened?) in which you used a you-message. Next, write the you-message you used. Watch for the words "should," "must," "ought to," "need to," "always," and "never." When you see one, circle it.

My You-Message Diary		
	Situation	You-message
Monday		
Tuesday		
Wednesday		
Thursday		
Friday		
Saturday		
Sunday		

In what situations do you most often use a you-message?

_____

_____

When you tried to use an I-message and it didn't work, what do you think made it difficult?

_____

_____

26 clear communication sends the correct message

for you to know

Misinterpretation or jumping to the wrong conclusion often results in hurt feelings and needless arguments—not to mention a lot of stress and worry. Clear communication depends not only on speakers sending the correct message but also on listeners checking that they have the correct information before reacting. When you're listening to friends, family members, or teachers, checking your conclusions is an easy way to avoid the misunderstandings that cause stress and worry.

Denise rushed home because her father was leaving on a business trip and she wouldn't see him for a month. She wanted to say goodbye and drive with her parents to the airport. As Denise walked into the kitchen, her mom said, "Hi, sweetie. You're home from school early. Is everything okay?" Denise thought, "She doesn't trust me. She thinks I cut my last class of the day," but decided to check this with her mom. "Mom, I know I'm home a little early. Do you think I cut my final class?" Denise was glad she checked her conclusion. Her mom replied, "No, sweetie. I was concerned that you might not be feeling well. You were up late last night and you said you felt really stressed. Are you okay?"

for you to do

Describe a time when you jumped to a conclusion before checking whether it was true. What was the situation? What happened?

_____

_____

_____

_____

_____

If you could go back and check the conclusion before you reacted, what questions could you have asked?

_____

_____

_____

_____

_____

more to do

Sometimes you cannot immediately check your conclusions because the other person isn't there. When this happens, you can think through other conclusions or ways of looking at the event. Just like where you sit in a movie theater gives you a slightly different view of the screen, you can have different views of a situation that can stress or calm you. Considering other ways to think about a situation can help you let go of a conclusion that is bothering you.

Describe a situation recently that bothered you (for example, when one of your friends didn't respond immediately to your text). List all the possible ways you could interpret this event.

_____

_____

_____

_____

What situations tend to cause you to quickly jump to a conclusion before you have all the facts?

_____

_____

_____

_____

for you to know

It's stressful when people add things to your plate when it's already filled with too many things to do. An overfull plate increases your stress, particularly when you have trouble saying no to someone who wants to add more to it. Learning to say no will help you feel less powerless when people ask you to do more and you're already doing a lot.

Juan's plate was very full. He had a big chemistry exam to study for, and he wanted to spend more time preparing for the debate in history class. Also, it was his mom's birthday, and he and his sisters wanted to give her a big party. Juan was already feeling overwhelmed by the number of things on his plate when Ms. Chan, his favorite teacher, asked whether he would be willing to tutor a couple of her students in math this week. Juan thought, "I can't say no to Ms. Chan. She's done so much for me." Juan knew that saying no was the right thing to do, but he didn't know how to say it. Then he remembered the saying-no exercise that Mr. Bennett had taught in health class. Mr. Bennett said that saying no was sometimes hard, but that it was simple to do, and it was just four steps.

for you to do

When you're doing enough already and someone asks you to do more, follow these four steps to say no to the request:

Step 1: State the problem. It's important to describe the facts; for example, "I have to study for my chemistry exam, prepare for the class debate, and help my sisters with my mother's birthday party, and you've asked me to tutor some of your students."

Step 2: State how the problem makes you feel; for example, "I'm feeling overwhelmed by the number of things on my plate."

Step 3: Say no, or request a change; for example, "Although I would love to help you, I can't tutor your students this week. I could do it next week if that works for you."

Step 4: Get the buy-in; for example, "Would that work for you?" or "Would you do that for me?" or "Would that be okay?" The buy-in is important. It makes the other person have to say no to you. This final step puts you in a position of power rather than powerlessness.

Now you try it. Use the My Saying-No Worksheet below (or download a blank copy at http://www.newharbinger.com/40095). Think of a situation in which someone is adding things to your plate that you cannot do or don't wish to do. Describe the situation and then write each of the four steps. Now, in the "Put it all together" section of the worksheet, write the script (what you plan to say). Practice the script while standing in front of a mirror until you feel calm and confident.

My Saying-No Worksheet	
Situation that I want to say no to:	
Step 1: State the problem.	
Step 2: State how the problem makes you feel.	
Step 3: Say no, or request a change.	
Step 4: Get the buy-in.	
Put it all together:	

more to do

There are many situations in which saying no could help you feel less stressed. Circle any of the following situations in which you have trouble saying no.

Friends pushing you to skip class

Friends asking you to do their homework

Friends pushing you to take sides

Friends pushing you to do drugs

Other _____

Parents asking you to do a chore while you're in the middle of something else

Teachers asking you to do extra work without a good reason

Coaches pushing you to work harder when you're already overwhelmed

Adults pushing you to do something that makes you anxious

Other _____

Who are the people in your life who are good at saying no? What could you learn from these people? Are there times when they are more effective or less effective at saying no, and why do you think that is?

_____

_____

_____

_____

_____

Putting It Off Just Heaps It On

28 breaking it down to move things along

for you to know

When you're stressed out, it's harder to move things along. You convince yourself that you'll do it later when you have more time or energy. As you put things off, the stress builds, and as it builds, it becomes more difficult to keep moving the project along until you finish it. To lower the stress and keep a project moving along, learn to break a big project into smaller projects or steps.

Ross was stressing. He had to write a three-paragraph essay and he didn't know when he would have time to work on it. He had a soccer game and then soccer practice for the next two days. Also, he's president of the soccer club at school and tomorrow is the monthly meeting. He can't miss that. "I'll never get the essay done in time," he thought. He felt the knot in his stomach that he knew meant that his stress was building.

Then Ross had one of those "aha" moments. He sat down and started to break the essay project into small steps and wrote them down—read the instructions for the essay; skim the chapter that has to do with the essay; list the topic sentences for each paragraph; write the first paragraph; write the second paragraph; write the third paragraph; ask his mom to proof it; include her suggestions; spell-check it; and print it. As Ross started to break the project down, his stress level began to ease, and he began to relax a bit. He felt more confident that he would have plenty of time for the soccer game, the practice, the school meeting, and the essay too.

for you to do

Copy the worksheet below (or download a blank copy at http://www.newharbinger .com/40095) to use later. Reread Ross's story, and on the worksheet, list all the small steps he took in writing the essay. Also, write down other small steps that didn't occur to Ross. Now, estimate how much time you would give each step if you were writing the essay.

Breaking It Down	
Project:	
Step	Estimated Time to Complete Step

more to do

Use another blank copy of the worksheet. Think of a project that is stressing you out. It could be a school project, home project, or even a friend project (for example, making a special birthday card for your best friend). Break this project down into small steps, and write them on the worksheet.

Next, look at the steps. Ask yourself how confident (0 to 100 percent) you feel that you can and will complete the step the way you described it. Try for 90 percent confidence. If your confidence is less than 90 percent, break that small step into a couple of smaller steps. Keep breaking each step down until you have steps that you're 90 percent confident you'll start and complete.

How confident do you feel now that you have a plan that makes sense and that you can complete? What effect did this have on your stress level?

_____

_____

_____

cutting a corner to move things along 29

for you to know

If you're like most teens, you have more things to do than time to do them. This makes life stressful, particularly if it's difficult for you to cut a corner. Cutting the right corner at the right time can lower your stress. Learning to cut corners increases your efficiency, because the truth is, it's not necessary to do everything or to put the same amount of time and effort into everything.

for you to do

Deciding whether to cut a corner or not depends on whether cutting it results in small consequences or big consequences for you. Circle the situations where it makes sense to cut a corner.

Quickly proofread an email to a potential employer.

Proofread an email twelve times before sending to a potential employer.

Fold your socks quickly and put them away.

Fold and refold your socks until they are all folded exactly the same.

Get up two hours early in the morning so that you can spend an hour on your hair.

Spend no more than ten minutes on your hair and sleep in.

Spend no more than an hour writing a three-paragraph essay.

Spend three hours writing a three-paragraph essay.

Describe any activities that you believe are impossible to cut corners when doing.
Do your friends cut corners when they do these activities? If they do, what happens
to them?

_____

_____

_____

_____

_____

_____

_____

more to do

Look at the activities you listed. Have you ever, for any reason, been forced to cut a corner (for example, to finish a homework assignment more quickly than you liked because you had too much to do)?

Yes   No

When you cut the corner, other than feeling uncomfortable, did anything terrible happen?

Yes   No

Can you think of a time when you refused to cut a corner and it actually caused you to do a worse job? If so, describe it here.

_____

_____

_____

_____

_____

30 procrastinating less to stress less

for you to know

You've probably said to yourself, "I'll clean my room on Saturday," or "One more video and then I'll start my homework." Sometimes it's okay to put off a task. However, if you're a big-time procrastinator, you likely know that putting off tasks only increases your stress. Talking back to the thoughts that give you permission to procrastinate will help you start tasks sooner, which will help you worry less about whether you'll have time to complete the important tasks in your life.

Jake is a big-time procrastinator. He puts off homework, piano practice, and even taking a shower before bed. Jake doesn't understand how Ben, his best friend, seems to do things without putting them off, even things that are boring or stressful. Ben seems to just do it. Jake decided to ask Ben how he does this. Ben said, "I learned long ago that it's better to tell myself to do it now than it is to tell myself that it's okay to do it later."

for you to do

Look at the list below. These are typical thoughts teens have that give them permission to put things off. Place a check next to your typical permission thoughts and add those you often have that don't appear in the list.

Permission Thoughts	✓
I'll do it later.	
I'll do it when I know exactly how to do it.	
I'll do it when I have more time.	
I'll do it when I'm less tired.	
I'll do it after I do a little more research.	
I'll do it after I play this last video game (or watch this last show).	
I'll do it in the morning on the way to school. It won't take long.	
I'll feel more like doing it tomorrow.	
Other:	
Other:	
Other:	

Often, when teens give themselves permission to put things off, they experience consequences. What consequences have you experienced because you gave in to your permission thoughts and put things off?

_____

_____

_____

more to do

Look at your list of typical permission thoughts. What could you say that would challenge the permission thought so that you can move things ahead? For example, to the permission thought, "I'll do it after I do a little more research," you could say, "I'll start my essay now. As I write the essay, I'll learn whether it's necessary to do more research or not, and starting the essay now will help me know what research I really need."

Your Permission Thought	Your Move-It-Ahead Thought

Getting good at challenging permission thoughts doesn't happen overnight. Many of them have been rolling around in your head for years. It will take time to get good at not giving yourself permission to put things off. Sometimes teens feel a little stressed when they think about changing a pattern they have been in for years. Describe any concerns you have about challenging your permission thoughts.

_____

_____

_____

_____

If you never learn to challenge permission thoughts, in what ways might your life get harder or more stressful?

_____

_____

_____

_____

Managing Stress That Angers You So You Can Manage Anger That Stresses You

31 your sources of anger

for you to know

Everybody gets angry. Anger isn't necessarily bad except when it creates problems for you. Trying to keep the lid on your anger is stressful. Dealing with the consequences when the lid pops off your anger is stressful too. The first step in learning to manage your anger is to identify your anger buttons—the things that set you off.

for you to do

We all have things that push our anger buttons. On the next page are some examples of typical anger buttons for teens. Place a check next to yours or add other anger buttons you have that don't appear in the list.

Anger Buttons	✓
When I lose at a game or sport	
When someone accuses me of something that I didn't do	
When someone ridicules me, especially in front of my friends	
When someone ignores me	
When someone bullies me or one of my friends	
When someone borrows my things without asking first	
When someone makes repetitive noises	
When someone makes too much noise when I'm trying to concentrate	
When someone spreads rumors about me	
When someone yells or screams at me	
When someone calls me or a friend or family member a name	
When someone lectures me	
When someone bosses me around	
When someone treats me unfairly	
Other:	
Other:	
Other:	

What are your top three anger buttons?

_____

_____

_____

Do your friends or family members have the same anger buttons? Why do you think that is?

_____

_____

_____

more to do

It's not just words or actions that set you off. Thoughts that automatically enter your head can trigger anger too. For example, if your sister takes the last cookie without asking if you want it, you might think, "She's so selfish. All she cares about is herself." Trigger thoughts fall into three categories: (1) the thought that a person harmed or ridiculed you, (2) the thought that the person *deliberately* harmed or ridiculed you, and (3) the thought that the person *should* have acted differently.

Think back to a situation in which you felt very angry. Write the situation next to the category that it best fits.

Trigger Thought Category	Situation
The thought that a person harmed or ridiculed you	
The thought that the person *deliberately* harmed or ridiculed you	
The thought that the person *should* have acted differently	

Are there particular people in your life who trigger your anger? What anger trigger thoughts do you have about them?

_____

_____

_____

Who in your life seems to be cool and calm in situations that make you boil? What thoughts do you think this person has about the same situations that help him or her stay cool when you're boiling?

_____

_____

_____

for you to know

Anger is like a volcano. There are the first rumblings that an eruption is on the way, but even before that, the heat, deep down, is building: heat that you don't know is even there. It helps that anger builds in stages. When you know your anger stages and the stage you're in at the moment, you'll be able to cool the volcano before it erupts.

for you to do

There are three anger stages. First, your body is stressed or tense, perhaps because you're worried about exams or problems with friends, or because you haven't slept well for days. A stressed body sets the stage for anger. Second, an event or situation pushes your anger button. Third, anger thoughts automatically shoot through your mind.

Let's take a look at Jon's anger stages.

Stage 1. Jon's body is tense.

Jon's plate is too full. He has a big exam tomorrow but he doesn't have much time to study because he has rugby practice after school. Also, Jon and his girlfriend had a big argument today, and she has been texting him all day long. He's stressed and just wants to relax before he starts his homework.

Stage 2. His sister pushes Jon's anger button.

As Jon walks into the house, his mom tells him that they're leaving for his grandmother's birthday party in thirty minutes. Jon then sees his older sister walk out the door. As she leaves, he asks, "Where are you going?" and his sister says, "To hang out with friends."

Stage 3. Jon's anger thought automatically shoots through his mind.

"My parents always give her a pass. It's not fair. They know how stressed I am and they don't care."

Jon's volcano is rumbling. It's only a matter of time before he explodes. Which category does Jon's anger trigger thought fit?

_____

_____

_____

Let's give Jon a redo. Based on what you've learned in the workbook so far, what could Jon do in each stage of his anger to cool down the volcano?

Stage 1. First, Jon could relax his tense and stressed-out body. For example, he could try slow deep breathing (activity 5) for ten minutes. How about progressive muscle relaxation (activity 6) every night to relax his body after a stressful day?

_____

_____

_____

_____

Stage 2. Second, Jon could identify what triggered his anger. Sometimes it's difficult to clearly identify what sets people off but usually there's a pattern. Does Jon often feel angry when his parents treat him and his sister differently? What do you think?

_____

_____

_____

_____

Stage 3. Third, Jon could identify what he was thinking that made him feel so angry. Has he jumped to any conclusions here? Is he blaming people before he has all the facts?

_____

_____

_____

_____

more to do

You can defuse your anger reactions by identifying what was happening in each of your anger stages. Take a recent situation when your volcano erupted. Describe each stage of your anger. Next, describe what you could have done differently if you had a redo.

Situation	Stage 1. Was your body stressed and why?	Stage 2. Which anger button was pushed?	Stage 3. What anger trigger thought did you have?
What could you have done or thought to cool yourself down?			

Think of a time when you were angry but were able to cool things down. How did you do that?

_____

_____

_____

for you to know

How you interpret or think about something can make a big difference in whether you blow up or stay calm. Sometimes the action you take when you're frustrated can make things better or worse for you. Learning to change your thoughts and actions can cool you down when someone or something pushes your anger button.

for you to do

Here are a couple of examples of teens using coping thoughts and actions to stay cool.

Amar and a friend are standing in line to buy tickets for the movie. They're joking around when a woman cuts in front of them.

Anger Trigger Thought: *Amar immediately thinks, "Hey, that's not fair. She thinks that just because we're kids we don't have rights?"*

Coping Thought: *Amar says to himself, "This doesn't have anything to do with our rights or her rights. I bet she didn't even see us."*

Coping Action: *Amar asserts himself and says, "Excuse me, ma'am, but the line is behind us."*

Cassandra and Ainsley are hanging out between classes. Cassandra checks her phone and says, "Hey, Olivia's texting to remind us about her party." Ainsley checks her phone but doesn't see a text from Olivia.

Anger Trigger Thought: *Ainsley thinks, "Olivia doesn't want me at her party. She hates me."*

Coping Thought: *Ainsley says to herself, "Wow, I'm jumping to conclusions here. Yesterday, Olivia told me that she'd see me at her party. Maybe she forgot to put me in the group text."*

Coping Action: *Ainsley checks her conclusion with Cassandra. She asks, "Is my name in Olivia's group text?" Just then, Olivia's text arrives.*

Describe a recent situation that pushed your anger button.

_____

_____

_____

What was your anger trigger thought?

_____

_____

Next, describe a coping thought you could have used to keep your cool.

_____

_____

Could you have done something that would have helped? Describe this coping action.

_____

_____

more to do

Here are a few more examples of coping thoughts and coping actions. Place a check next to the ones you think would be helpful for you, and then add some of your own.

Coping Thoughts	✓
Blaming other people doesn't help. What can I do to change the situation?	
Maybe this isn't as bad as it feels.	
Am I seeing the whole picture?	
Am I sticking to the facts?	
Does it always or never happen?	
No one is right, no one is wrong. We just see things differently.	
I'm not going to let her get to me.	
I can't change him with anger.	
Other:	
Other:	
Other:	

Coping Action	✓
Problem solving (see activities 20, 21, and 22)	
Using I-messages (see activity 25)	
Saying no or asserting yourself (see activity 27)	
Slow deep breathing (see activity 5)	
Shift into automatic relaxation (see activity 7)	
Other:	
Other:	
Other:	

You probably have a friend who rarely blows up. Describe the coping thoughts and actions you think that friend uses to stay cool.

_____

_____

_____

for you to know

Creating an anger management plan helps you prepare for situations that tend to push your anger buttons. Once you have a clear plan of action, you'll want to test it to see whether it works. Having a plan you're confident about will help you cool down and worry less about unexpectedly blowing up.

for you to do

Before you begin this activity, make several copies of the blank My Anger-Management Plan worksheet below (or download a blank worksheet at http://www.newharbinger .com/40095). Now take three copies of the blank worksheet, and describe in the Anger Scene section three anger situations that regularly come up for you. Write it like a scene in a movie or story. Include details about what is happening, and what people are doing, saying, and feeling. In each situation, make sure to include your anger thoughts and the urges you feel to act in an angry way. Take a look at the plan that Abby came up with.

My Anger-Management Plan
Anger Rating (0–10, where 10 is extreme anger) 5
Anger Scene I'm at school when I see Mady hanging out with some other girls. They look at me and laugh, and that makes me start to boil with anger. I think, "They hate my new sweater. They're mocking me. They're talking about me and putting me down." Jessica waves at me, and I know she's just trying to make it look like they're not talking about me, but I know they are. I feel humiliated. The anger is building inside me. I have the urge to go over and tell them that I hate what they're wearing too.
Anger Trigger Thoughts "They're mocking me." "They're talking about me and putting me down."
Anger Coping Thoughts "Wow, I'm jumping to conclusions. I don't actually know what they're talking about." "I don't really like this sweater, so what's the big deal? Maybe they don't care about the sweater either." "Yesterday they complimented the blouse I was wearing, and Jessica asked me if she could borrow it one day."
Anger Coping Actions "I'll go over and say hi to Jessica. I've known her since first grade. I'll know pretty quickly whether she cares about what I'm wearing or not." "I'll take three slow deep breaths before I go over. That always helps me cool down."

Now you try it. Rate each of your three anger scenes on a 0 to 10 scale, where 10 is extreme anger and 0 is cool and calm. Write that number in the Anger Rating section. In the Anger Trigger Thoughts section, write the anger thoughts you likely would have in the scene. Last, in the Anger Coping Thoughts and Actions sections, write coping thoughts and coping actions that you think will help you cool down.

My Anger-Management Plan
Anger Rating (0–10, where 10 is extreme anger)   _____
Anger Scene
Anger Trigger Thoughts
Anger Coping Thoughts
Anger Coping Actions

more to do

Sit in a quiet comfortable place, and close your eyes. Once you're relaxed, imagine the anger scene you rated the lowest on the 0 to 10 scale. Try to imagine the scene in as much detail as possible. Imagine what people are saying or doing. Intensify your anger by thinking your anger trigger thoughts. Let your anger rise as much as you can. Set a timer for about a minute and then hold the scene in your mind. When the timer beeps, use your relaxation skills and your anger coping thoughts to decrease your anger. Keep this up until your anger drops back to zero. Repeat this process again, visualizing the anger scene and then switching to your anger management plan. Practice with the same anger scene for a few days, and then switch to the scene you rated next lowest on the 0 to 10 scale. Finally, switch to the scene you rated highest.

Describe what this was like for you. Were you surprised by how angry you felt just by imagining these anger scenes? What new anger thoughts came up for you while you visualized them?

_____

_____

_____

If you had trouble forming images of anger scenes, include more physical and sensory (sounds, smells) pieces to the scene. Rewrite your anger scene and try again.

Imagining the anger trigger scenes and using your anger management plan will increase your confidence that you can manage your anger in typical situations that cause you to boil.

Eating Right, Eating Well—Just Try Not to Eat to Calm Down

35 your eating right, eating well profile

for you to know

When stressed, some teens tend to eat high-fat, high-calorie food and to eat too much of it. Other teens skip meals when they're stressed. Eating, or not eating, to manage your emotions isn't healthy for your body or mind. Both patterns can cause you to feel tired and irritable, to have trouble focusing and thinking clearly, and to have less motivation to work on what is stressing you out in the first place.

Ayesha is worrying big time. She just found out that she has three major assignments due next week and not much time to study because all weekend she'll be driving her brother to and from his baseball tournament. When Ayesha gets stressed, she finds comfort in snacking on junk food. She snacks during breaks at school and in the evening when she's doing homework. Because she is so stressed, Ayesha barely notices when and what she's eating. The junk food makes her feel sluggish and distracted, and now she is having an even harder time completing her work. As Ayesha feels more sluggish and gets further behind, her stress and worry increase.

for you to do

To create an eating right, eating well profile, take a look at how stress impacts what, when, and how you eat. Let's start with what you eat. Describe what you eat when you feel stressed and when you feel relaxed.

_____

_____

_____

Next describe when you eat (for example, when doing homework, at school on the day of a big test). If you eat at different times when you're stressed, write that down as well.

_____

_____

_____

Lastly, describe how you eat. Do you eat breakfast sitting down, or while on the go, such as while riding the bus to school? Do you eat alone while worrying about an upcoming test or with friends relaxing and having fun?

_____

_____

_____

more to do

To best understand how unhealthy eating impacts your stress, energy, and mood, complete the exercise below. Understanding this connection illustrates the feedback loop between diet and worry.

When I eat unhealthy:

My stress level will:	√	My energy level will:	√	I feel: (Check all that apply)	√
Decrease a lot		Decrease a lot		Happy	
Decrease a little		Decrease a little		Sad	
Stay the same		Stay the same		Angry	
Increase a little		Increase a little		Frustrated	
Increase a lot		Increase a lot		Guilty	
				Other:	

developing your eating right, eating well plan 36

for you to know

Following an eating right, eating well plan will help give you the energy you need to work on reducing your stress. It will help you avoid or break the cycle where stress eating leads to more stress and less energy. Your body will have the fuel it needs.

for you to do

In this activity, you'll learn the three basics of healthy eating and develop an eating right, eating well plan.

Basic 1: Think about moderation.

Moderation means avoiding excess or extremes. You might be tempted to set strict rules or have no rules for food to control your stress level. Strict or no rules don't usually work and lead to unhealthy choices, which is why moderation is so important.

Basic 2: Eat healthy foods first.

Your body runs on food like a car runs on gas. Not eating isn't an option, and filling the tank with mainly low-grade fuel will make your car run poorly or even break down. Fill your tank with healthy foods first; then there will be less room for unhealthy foods. Start with colorful fruits and vegetables. Top off the tank, if you wish, with foods with less color, those beige and brown chips and cookies. Remember though, food companies know the trick about color. Start with foods that naturally have color rather than foods that color has been added to, such as chips.

Basic 3: Pay attention to how you eat and not just what you eat.

Mindful eating is when you pay close attention to what you're eating. It can help you with portion control, which is key to moderation. Mindful eating also makes you less likely to race past the "tank-is-full" warning your stomach sends to your brain when you have eaten enough. In order to eat more mindfully, don't read, text, or watch videos while you eat. If you're eating, just eat. It's also helpful to sit down when you eat. Sitting down, rather than eating on the go, can remind you to eat at a slower pace and pay attention to when your tank feels full.

Now, use the three basics to create your eating right, eating well plan for the week. For each basic, set a goal for the week:

Moderation Goal

Example: *Instead of making certain foods off limits, which will only make my body crave them more, I will save dessert for when I go out with friends or family this weekend.*

_____

_____

_____

Healthy Foods First Goal

Example: *I will keep healthy snacks in my backpack or in my locker so I can easily reach for them first.*

_____

_____

_____

Mindful Eating Goal

Example: *I will eat breakfast without my phone or any other distraction. I will eat slowly and will not do anything else but eat.*

_____

_____

_____

more to do

For the following week, use the table below (or download Tracking My Eating Goals at http://www.newharbinger.com/40095) to chart your progress. Write your three goals, and add a check for each day you successfully accomplished that goal.

Tracking My Eating Goals			
Day	Moderation Goal	Healthy Food First Goal	Mindful Eating Goal
Monday			
Tuesday			
Wednesday			
Thursday			
Friday			
Saturday			
Sunday			

Exercising Your Way to Less Stress

37 selecting the best exercise for you

for you to know

Exercise is great for reducing stress. People who exercise regularly feel more relaxed, more confident, and better about themselves; and when you exercise, it doesn't take long for you to reap these benefits. You feel better immediately after exercise and better throughout the day. Regular exercise is a great buffer against stress and usually costs you nothing but a little time.

Although Ezra likes to stay active all year round, his junior year was tough and stressful, and he thought he was just too busy to exercise during the first semester. Once lacrosse practice began in January, Ezra started exercising again. At the end of the school year, Ezra realized something: while he had a lot more to do second semester with lacrosse practices and games, SAT preparation, and the usual homework, his overall stress was lower and his mood was better during that period.

for you to do

The best exercise is one that you enjoy and that you'll do regularly. If it fits into your daily life or is an activity you really like, you're more likely to do it. Large exercises tend to take time and often require you starting small and building up your endurance. Also, some large exercises require other people, such as tennis. Below is a list of large exercises. Check the best one for you, and add your own ideas.

Large Exercises	✓
Biking	
Hiking	
Running	
Skateboarding	
Swimming	
Team sports (Write down examples.)	
Walking	
Working out at a gym	
Yoga	
Other:	
Other:	
Other:	

more to do

Make exercise fit into your day rather than trying to fit the day into your exercise plan. Small exercises are easier because they take less time and don't require equipment or teammates. For example, walking is a great way to exercise. If you walk to class, take the long way. If your mom asks you to go to the store for milk, walk there if you can. Volunteer to carry the laundry upstairs or walk the dog. Stand rather than sit, and stretch while you do other things. You can also do the things you already do but try to do them faster, such as running home from the bus stop rather than walking. Below is a list of small exercises. Check the best one for you, and add your own ideas.

Small Exercises	✓
Cleaning your house	
Dancing in the shower	
Dancing while getting dressed	
Doing active video games (Kinect)	
Exercising during TV or radio ads	
Parking your car a few blocks from school and walking	
Stretching between classes	
Walking your dog (or just going on a walk)	
Other:	
Other:	

developing your exercise plan 38

for you to know

"Just do it" might be a great slogan for a shoe company, but it's not that simple when it comes to sustaining an exercise habit. There are many reasons it's difficult to keep your intention to exercise regularly. Some people expect it will be easy to exercise every day and feel discouraged when they miss a day or two. Others stop exercising because they believe they're just too busy. Regardless of the reasons, an exercise plan will help.

for you to do

Building an exercise plan comes down to four basics: plan, partner, proclaim, and praise.

Basic 1: Plan

Begin with a schedule that is specific, flexible, and practical. What is the most convenient time for you to exercise? What time of day do you feel most motivated to work out? When during the day could you include small exercise activities?

Basic 2: Partner

It's much easier to build an exercise habit when you do it with a buddy. Even if your buddy exercises with you only once a week, the structure and motivation will help. If your friend isn't available to exercise with you, ask her to text you when she completes her exercise, and you do the same.

Basic 3: Proclaim

Tell friends and family members about your exercise plan and announce to them when you walk out the door to jog, or when you're headed to dance. Texting them can work too. Public proclamations motivate us and set us up for congratulations and praise from others when we follow through with our exercise.

Basic 4: Praise

Building and sustaining an exercise habit isn't easy. You deserve credit each time you exercise, even a little. If you walked around the block and volunteered to walk the dog twice this week, don't be hard on yourself if you didn't get around to playing basketball with a friend too. Praise yourself for what you did, even if you did a little less than you intended to do.

Now follow the basics to create your exercise plan.

Plan: Make enough copies of this schedule (or download the worksheet My Exercise Schedule at http://www.newharbinger.com/40095) to use over the next few months with the exercises you selected in activity 37. Include a large exercise and a small exercise. Place a check next to the exercise when you do it.

My Exercise Schedule				
Day	Large Exercise	✓	Small Exercise	✓
Monday				
Tuesday				
Wednesday				
Thursday				
Friday				
Saturday				
Sunday				

Partner: On the lines below, write the names of three possible exercise partners:

_____

_____

_____

Proclaim: On the lines below, write the names of people you'll tell about your intention to exercise:

_____

_____

_____

Praise: Each week, add the total number of checks, and give yourself credit for what you accomplished. Perhaps you'd like to watch your favorite show or treat yourself and a friend to a movie over the weekend. Also, remember to be a good coach to yourself. On the lines below, write what you'll tell yourself when you exercise that will help you feel good about what you did:

_____

_____

_____

more to do

Setting realistic exercise goals can help maintain your motivation and prevent you from getting discouraged. To set realistic exercise goals, it's important to know your starting point. After two weeks of practicing the above exercise plan, evaluate how things have gone:

Week 1:   Number of large exercises: _____

Number of small exercises: _____

Week 2:   Number of large exercises: _____

Number of small exercises: _____

Try to set new goals based on how the first two weeks went. Set goals either at or only slightly higher than what you have been doing until you reach a point you're happy with. You may remember from earlier in the workbook that a realistic goal is a goal you're 90 percent confident that you can and will complete. Write down your goal for the next few weeks below:

_____

_____

_____

Space Matters: Creating a Calm Environment

39 creating a calming space

for you to know

In ancient days, human survival depended on a safe and secure environment, and this hasn't changed much. We feel more comfortable in some environments and less comfortable in others, and we tend to seek out comforting spaces when we are stressed and anxious. There are many ways that you can transform a space into a calm and soothing place to study and hang out with friends.

When Matias arrived home after a stressful day, he headed straight to his bedroom. On less stressful days, he might hang out with his mom in the kitchen, or if his brother was home, shoot some baskets with him in the backyard. However, when he was stressed about a test, upset with a friend, or worried about an upcoming presentation at school, he made a beeline to his room. Although Matias knew he felt better in his bedroom, he had never considered why he tended to head there when he was feeling stressed.

for you to do

Most likely, your calming space is your bedroom. There are some basics to creating a calming space, such as making it orderly and quiet, but otherwise, there is a ton of room to make a space that reflects your unique tastes and personality.

Let's start with the basics—*order* and *quiet*. Order is the key to a stress-free bedroom. If you take the time to return things back to their homes (and once you have organized your room the first time, it won't take much time later), you won't feel stressed about losing your things or race around in the morning before school trying to find them.

Sit in the doorway of your bedroom and look around you. Are things where they belong? On the lines below, write what you could do to organize your room. For example, if your earbuds or jewelry are on the floor or lost in a mess on the bedside table, you could install some neat and inexpensive hooks on the walls and hang them there.

_____

_____

_____

_____

_____

The next basic is quiet. On the lines below, write the things you could do to make your room quieter. For example, if your bedroom is near the living room where there's lots of noise, you could play music (calming music is best) or turn on a fan to drown out the noise, or place rugs on wooden floors to quiet things down a bit.

_____

_____

_____

_____

_____

more to do

Once you have added the basics to your space, there are many other things you can do to create a calming space. Could you bring a couple of plants into your space or move your desk in front of a window so that you can look at a tree or garden? Could you paint your room in some soothing colors (earth tones are best)? Brainstorm the changes to your room that would make it a soothing and calming space. Then, in the space below, draw your room and where you placed things to make it a calming space.

To help you plan the changes to your room, organize the changes to your space in terms of cost and difficulty:

Easy to Change	Inexpensive to Change
Difficult to Change	**Expensive to Change**

For things that are difficult and expensive to change, think about easier and less expensive options and write them on the lines below.

_____

_____

_____

_____

_____

40 harnessing the power of your calming space

for you to know

Over the years, your space likely has become linked to the stress that comes with homework, deadlines, and difficult texts with friends. In order to break this link, it's necessary to build a new link that pairs relaxation rather than stress with your space. Once you build this connection, hanging out in your space will help you relax and stay calm, even during stressful times.

for you to do

The first step is to organize your space into stress-free zones. A great stress-free zone is your bed. The last thing you want to feel is stress when you're lying in bed and waiting for sleep to come. List your other stress-free zones.

_____

_____

_____

Use the stress-free zones for stress-free activities only. For example, if you have designated your bed as a stress-free zone, don't study there and don't speak to friends there if you're anticipating a difficult conversation. That means do your homework somewhere else, unless homework doesn't stress you out at all. Next, list the places in your space that are stress zones, but that you would like to make into stress-free zones.

_____

_____

_____

more to do

After two weeks, describe what it was like for you to protect your stress-free zones. Did you enjoy the space more? Did you feel more relaxed than usual there?

_____

_____

_____

Describe what it was like for you to feel relaxed in your stress zones.

_____

_____

_____

wrapping up

In this workbook, there are forty activities that teach skills to help you relax and reduce stress. Decades of research demonstrate that these skills work. But like any skill, they work only if you practice, and practice enough until you use the skills automatically without thinking, particularly when you're feeling stressed and anxious. It's just like in soccer or basketball: in order to pass the ball in the right direction and at the right time and to do this without thinking, it's necessary to practice the skill over and over and over. Activity 3, Creating Your Game Plan, will help you set up a practice plan and stay at it.

Building any habit, even the relaxation and stress reduction habit, isn't a straight line. There are ups and downs, and plateaus when you feel stuck. In fact, getting stuck is normal. The trick is to get unstuck quickly and a plan can help. In the future, if you feel stuck, download a copy of the worksheet Getting Unstuck at http://www.newharbinger.com/40095 and use it. It will help you quickly get back on track practicing and using your relaxation and stress reduction skills.

Certain skills in this workbook will work better for you than others. It's okay to have your favorites. However, if you're feeling particularly stressed, and your favorite skills don't seem to be enough, review the workbook and try some of the others. A workbook with forty skills means that you're likely to find one or two more skills that help.

Although we've written this workbook for teens, this doesn't mean that the skills in the workbook won't help when you're older. Every change and every challenge, whether in college or in your first job, brings some stress and anxiety. The relaxation and stress reduction skills that helped you in your teen years will help you then, and for many years to come.

acknowledgments

We wish to thank Matthew McKay, who—along with his coauthors Martha Davis and Elizabeth Robbins Eshelman—invented the wheel when he wrote and published *The Relaxation and Stress Reduction Workbook*, now in its sixth edition, for an adult audience. Our book simply rotated the wheels slightly to fit a different model: teens.

We wish to thank Emily Berner, Joan Davidson, Daniela Owen, and Monique Thompson at the San Francisco Bay Area Center for Cognitive Therapy. They are superb clinician-scientists as well as thoughtful and caring colleagues. We appreciate their ongoing support of our professional development, including our writing of this book.

We wish to extend a special thank-you to Tesilya Hanauer, acquisitions manager at New Harbinger Publications. Her thoughtful feedback improved the overall quality of the manuscript and our confidence in the final product. We also thank the other members of the New Harbinger Publications team who were unwaveringly patient and professional.

Every teen is different but all are smart, resourceful, and amazing. With each teen, we learn something to help the next one. Thanks for passing it on.

We wish to thank our families for their support and encouragement of this project. We cannot imagine how we could have completed this book without you.

Michael A. Tompkins, PhD, ABPP, is codirector of the San Francisco Bay Area Center for Cognitive Therapy; assistant clinical professor at the University of California, Berkeley; and a diplomate and founding fellow of the Academy of Cognitive Therapy. Tompkins specializes in the treatment of anxiety disorders and obsessive-compulsive spectrum disorders in adults, adolescents, and children. He is author or coauthor of numerous articles on cognitive behavioral therapy (CBT) and related topics, as well as seven books, including three books published by New Harbinger Publications: *Digging Out*, *OCD: A Guide for the Newly Diagnosed*, and *Anxiety and Avoidance*. Tompkins serves on the advisory board of Magination Press, the children's press of the American Psychological Association. He is a certified supervisor and trainer for the Beck Institute for Cognitive Behavior Therapy and the Academy of Cognitive Therapy. Tompkins has been featured in *The New York Times*, *The Wall Street Journal*, on NPR, and has presented over 250 workshops, lectures, and keynote addresses on CBT and related topics.

Jonathan R. Barkin, PsyD, is a licensed clinical psychologist, partner at the San Francisco Bay Area Center for Cognitive Therapy, and assistant clinical professor at the University of California, Berkeley. Barkin has extensive experience in the treatment of severe anxiety disorders. He specializes in the treatment of anxiety disorders and obsessive-compulsive spectrum disorders in children, teens, and adults. Barkin presents lectures and workshops to professionals in the San Francisco Bay Area.

Foreword writer **Matthew McKay, PhD**, is a professor at the Wright Institute in Berkeley, CA. He has authored or coauthored numerous books, including *The Relaxation and Stress Reduction Workbook*, *Self-Esteem*, *Thoughts and Feelings*, *When Anger Hurts*, and *ACT on Life Not on Anger*. McKay received his PhD in clinical psychology from the California School of Professional Psychology, and specializes in the cognitive behavioral treatment of anxiety and depression. He lives and works in the greater San Francisco Bay Area.

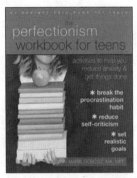

Register your **new harbinger** titles for additional benefits!

When you register your **new harbinger** title—purchased in any format, from any source—you get access to benefits like the following:

- Downloadable accessories like printable worksheets and extra content

- Instructional videos and audio files

- Information about updates, corrections, and new editions

Not every title has accessories, but we're adding new material all the time.

Access free accessories in 3 easy steps:

1. Sign in at NewHarbinger.com (or **register** to create an account).

2. Click on **register a book**. Search for your title and click the **register** button when it appears.

3. Click on the **book cover or title** to go to its details page. Click on **accessories** to view and access files.

That's all there is to it!

If you need help, visit:

NewHarbinger.com/accessories

new harbinger
CELEBRATING
40 YEARS